5 Steps to Better Audiobooks:
An Indie Author's Guide to Awesome Audio Productions

By Julie C. Gilbert

Illustrated by Tim Sparvero

Aletheia Pyralis Publishers

For information about special discounts available for bulk purchases, sales promotions, fund-raising and educational needs, please email: juliecgilbert5steps@gmail.com.

http://www.juliecgilbert.com/

https://sites.google.com/view/juliecgilbert-writer/

Not ready to dive into Audiobooks stuff?

Love Science Fiction or Mystery?

Choose your adventure!
Visit: http://www.juliecgilbert.com/

For details on getting free books.

Endorsement:

"Audiobook creation is a funny little world, full of clustered people passionately doing their own thing, and reaching out to strangers on the internet for help. It can feel incredibly disjointed. What Julie Gilbert has done here is show us how to produce an audiobook with great detail, room for options, kindness, and community." ~ Kae Marie Denino, Narrator

Dedication:

To the lovely narrators I've worked with—Kristin Condon, Caitlin Jacques, Reuben Corbett, E. Roy Worley, Julie Hinton, L.W. Salinas, Rick Struve, Brian Troxell, Elizabeth Perry, Jacqueline DeGraff, Curt Bonnem, Liz Brand—and the many more I hope to work with someday.

Special Thanks:
To Tim Sparvero for the wonderful illustrations.
To the narrators who answered my many questions.
To the many beta readers—especially Julie Hinton and Kae Denino—for excellent feedback.

Table of Contents:

Introduction:

Dear Author (or other party interested in what it takes to commission an audiobook),

Who is this book for and how should you use it?

The main target audience for this book is independent or small press authors who wish to take their books into the audiobook arena. I hope guiding you through the audiobook process will help you avoid common pitfalls and make the most of the journey. Other interested parties who might get something out of reading this are new or would-be narrators, small publishers, and personal assistants to any of the above. If you're fortunate enough to land with a big publishing house, they probably have their own process for creating audiobooks.

Ideally, you should check out this book before jumping into audiobook publishing, but if you're in the starting stages and feeling overwhelmed, then it's still applicable. In most of the 5 Steps series of books, I begin with the steps and expand to other topics later, but this round, I believe there's a lot more background to give before exploring the steps.

You could skip right to the 5 steps, but if this is your first experience with making audiobooks, I recommend working from the beginning. While audio is a totally awesome format to experience books in, as a learning tool, it may be better for you to work with the ebook or a paperback version, whichever allows you to comfortably take notes in.

If you can avoid a perfectly awful first experience, you may find that you'll want to turn your entire backlog into audiobooks.

Who am I and why should you care what I have to say?

I'm an independently published author who writes both fiction and nonfiction. By the time this book goes to print, I should have at least twenty-six titles in audiobook format with another few in the works. Those numbers will hopefully be horribly outdated in a matter of years. Point being, I've learned a lot along the way.

In addition, I'm also high school chemistry teacher, so I know the value of having information in multiple mediums. My goal is for you to integrate the lessons I've learned into your own system for getting your books turned into audiobooks.

Limitations and Scope:

I've used Amazon's Audiobook Creation Exchange (ACX) more than twenty-five times. Therefore, most of my advice will be geared for producing an audiobook through that platform. That said, I have also tried Findaway Voices once, and I know there are other audiobook publishers out there. I can't really address them because I know little more than what Google can tell me.

Despite being comfortable with public speaking, I lack the acting skills to narrate my own books. That would certainly save me a lot of money, but I have no desire to learn the technical side of the business either. If you really wish to break it down, you need the written material, the ability to deliver a clear performance, the equipment to do the recording, and the software and technical knowhow to edit the files properly. Please don't take this to mean that it can't be done and done well, but this isn't a book about how to narrate a story yourself or how to become a narrator. It's a book (by a writer) primarily for authors who wish to hire a narrator.

The only other book of this nature I found in a super-quick search of Amazon was written by a narrator. It's probably an awesome book, but if you've ever lurked in some author or narrator Facebook groups, you'll know the concerns of authors and narrators can differ. A few people can do it all, but many more are only writers or narrators or technical service providers. It's tempting to let this become an us vs. them thing, but I hope to show you how to form the type of strong relationships with your narrator that will foster the creation of awesome audiobooks.

What's in this book?

I'm going to start by discussing the many lessons I've learned from commissioning audiobooks. Next, I'll list 4 reasons to jump right in, describe 3 reality checks, and answer 3 money-related questions briefly. Following that, I'll expand on the money question discussion from three different angles. Chapter 6 will be an overview of my personal process for getting a book to audio format. Chapters 7-11 will be an in-depth look at each of the 5 steps to better audiobooks. Finally, I'll close it out with some do's and don'ts if you want narrators to like you, a primer on audiobook promotions, the basics of email communication with your narrator, and seeing the situation from both sides.

5 Steps to Better Audiobooks:

Step #1: Choose your path (and book) wisely
Step #2: Select a strong audition script (or two) and do some narrator homework
Step #3: Choose a great narrator
Step #4: Maintain clear lines of communication
Step #5: Do a final review (or two)

Disclaimer 1:

I would love to guarantee that following these steps will ensure a smooth, painless experience, but life can—and often will—get in the way. I can only say that the 5 steps will increase the likelihood of making the journey smoother for you.

Disclaimer 2:

You may find sections of this book repetitive. That's partly by design, as this is mainly aimed at authors at several stages of the audiobook creation experience. The 5 steps sections will have more details, but there are some informational chapters first to introduce the topics.

Conclusion:

If I haven't scared you off yet, welcome. Creating audiobooks can be addictive, so be prepared for that aspect. No matter what your financial situation may be, if you have the desire to do this, it can be done.

Chapter 1:
Lessons Learned from 25$^+$ Audio Adventures

Introduction:

There's no getting around the fact that I've made mistakes throughout my journey to publish my stories as audiobooks. The good news for you is that you can learn from my experiences and hopefully not repeat them.

First, some abbreviations and definitions:

- **Audiobook Creation Exchange (ACX)** – Amazon's platform for making audiobooks; it's useful in allowing authors and narrators to find each other
- **Rights Holder** – Most likely you, the author or publisher
- **Narrator** – Somebody you hire to be the voice of your story. Sometimes, the narrator handles the production end as well.
- **Producer/Editor** – These are two separate jobs but often held by the same person. Some narrators also handle the production side, but outsourcing is also common. This person handles making the audiobook, which includes recording and editing the files.
- **Royalty Share (RS)** – a system of payment where the author and narrator split the royalties from each sale

- **Per Finished Hour (PFH)** – a system of payment where the author or other rights holder pays the narrator a set amount for each hour of finished audiobook
- **Royalty Share Plus (RS+)** – ACX's bid to standardize hybrid deals; the rights holder will pay the narrator something in addition to sharing the royalties from sales
- **Voices Share** – Findaway Voices's bid to standardize hybrid deals

Lesson 1: Review everything multiple times!

It's a BIG pain to get a production changed after you've approved it. Check, double check, and triple check the quality, no matter how long it takes. Somehow, one of my books ended up with the prologue repeated twice instead of Chapter 1 being present. Since I didn't have the files, I had to rely upon the producer to fix it. The problem took about six months to fix. There's a method to the madness of how many times I review the files these days.

Lesson 2: ACX deadlines are fluid if you and the narrator agree.

They're only guidelines. I always ask the narrator what timeline they want in the contract, but very few of them have ever stuck to those deadlines. It's taken everything from a few weeks to a couple of years to finish some of these projects. On the flip side, I've had many of them turn in the project before the deadline because they wisely built in some wiggle room.

Lesson 3: Casting your narrator is critically important.

I once cast a male narrator for a book that was largely first-person perspective from two teenage girls. It didn't even occur to me until he read part of the manuscript and was like "Uh, you probably want a woman to narrate this."

Incidentally, you can change narrators. As long as everybody agrees, ACX lets you drop previous contracts and create new ones. That's how we solved this issue. I had a woman cast for a different book, so they switched. The other project had a female protagonist too, but the point of view was third person. The male narrator dropped out much later for a different reason, but I found a nice lady to pick up the contract.

My point is that choosing the right voice for your book often begins with the question of whether you want a man or a woman to narrate. That question is devilishly hard to answer for nonfiction projects. When I opened auditions for *5 Steps to Surviving Chemistry* and *5 Steps to Better Blurbs*, I accepted entries from both men and women. Both books could easily have gone either way, but it happened that the former one went to a man and the latter went to a woman.

Julie C. Gilbert

Don't be afraid to go with your gut:

Besides the basics, make sure the voice fits the character. I recently went through thirty auditions on one project, and I had several viable candidates. The woman I hired simply fit the character better than the others. Every top candidate could have done a fine job with the project. The same held true for casting the Shadow Council series. The woman hired had a naturally lower-pitched voice, which I felt fit the main character—an FBI agent—better than some of the others.

Lesson 4: Communication is crucial.

I can't emphasize that point enough. It's also a tricky point because communication's a two-way street. You can only provide one half of the equation. When I describe my process about connecting with narrators, you'll see some ways that will help with estimating how good your prospective narrator is at communicating, but it's not foolproof.

If they have questions about anything, you should be very responsive and thorough with your answers. The clearer your instructions, the better the narrator will understand the project, and the less work there will be for both of you later. When I asked narrators what they'd like from the rights holders, they quite often said better communication.

Lesson 5: Explore your options.

ACX used to be the only major player in the audiobook creation game, but over the years, it's gotten some competition. The most promising of these is Findaway Voices. I only used them once because I like being more hands-on with narrator selection and file review, but if you're starting out, you may like the fact that they handle more things for you.

Conclusion:

Producing audiobooks is addictive, satisfying, and loads of fun. You should totally go for it. There are many things to consider throughout the process of getting books from words on a page to sweet sounds in listeners' ears.

Chapter 2:
4 Reasons, 3 Reality Checks, 3 Answers

Introduction:

If you're reading—or listening to—this book, you probably don't need much convincing in the "you should get your book into audio format" department. Nevertheless, I'll start this section by exploring some of the reasons people have for pursuing this medium. To balance things out, I'll also provide a short list of reality checks before briefly talking about money.

4 Reasons to Jump In:

1. New experience:

Even if you decide to read the book yourself, audiobooks are a separate experience than e-books or paperbacks or even movies and TV shows. Each medium tells a story in a slightly different way.

I find no reason for audiobooks to be in direct competition with their "bookish" counterparts, e-books and paperbacks. They're just different. While I don't quite hop on board with those who love reading e-books along with the audio version, I'm a huge fan of the format. Personally, it comes down to saving time.

Are audiobooks really timesavers?
This point is up for debate. Some people possess the ability to read at unholy speeds. I'm officially jealous of such people. Many who fall into this category don't enjoy audiobooks because they can finish the story much faster than the narrator. Others like audiobooks because they can be enjoyed during long commutes and while doing other tasks.

Side note: I've discovered this lovely thing at the bottom of most apps for playing back audiobooks. It changes the speed. Don't tell the narrators, but often, I listen to books using the 2x feature. 2.5x and 3x are also useful, but 3.5x gives me a headache. If you're looking for straight book consumption maximization, changing the speed can help. Understand that the downside of messing with the track speed is that it destroys many of the nuances of the performance.

How do audiobooks enhance the "reading" experience?
Every person who answers this question will come up with something different.

Top 5 personal reasons to love audiobooks:
> #1: Some audiobooks use sound effects very well. (On the other hand, for every book that uses sound effects well, a dozen more use them horribly.)
> #2: It's easier to have somebody read the book to you.
> #3: A talented narrator can bring the characters to life.
> #4: Some dialogue lines are more powerful when read aloud.
> #5: I love being able to multitask. It makes me feel like I can squeeze in so many more stories than I would be able to if I had to find real reading time. My favorite times for listening to audiobooks are ironing, walking, and driving.

- **Bonus reason:** You can experience audiobooks with other people. (I don't do this, but I like that there's that option.)

Julie C. Gilbert

2. Support other artists and make friends:
This doesn't apply if you intend to read the book yourself, unless you really want to stretch the meaning. I find great satisfaction in supporting emerging narrators through the audiobook process. Don't get me wrong, I also enjoy working with established narrators who know the ropes already. There's something wonderful about the discovery process, though that might just be the science teacher in me.

During the audition process, you will likely get to interact with more than a dozen narrators at various stages of their career. Once you choose someone, you should work very closely with this person to see that the story vision is realized. I am not saying you'll immediately have an instant connection and be best friends, but I have made a few good friends over the years. I never would have met them if I didn't hire them to voice one of my books.

3. Sell more books:
Sometimes, one must state the obvious. The writing life in general isn't solely about the money. If you want to fight me on that point, read the reality checks first, then we can chat. The more formats you have a book in, the more opportunities you have to sell it.

Increase the accessibility of your books:
Sharing a story is a fun part of the process. It's nice to be able to reach people however they like absorbing books. I recently spent some time re-publishing some of my Heartfelt Cases books in large print to increase the reach and accessibility. For some, audiobooks are the only way they're able to experience stories.

4. Creating an audiobook is highly satisfying:
There's a reason you became a writer. You love stories. Creating an audiobook takes time, effort, and in many cases, money, but like most other things requiring those ingredients, it's worth it. You love the characters, but have you heard their voices in your head? Through the audio version, your story comes off the page and goes directly into the hearts and minds of readers.

12

Many writers have dreams of having their books turned into movies. While audiobooks aren't movies, they involve a performance aspect. The physical hurdles and budget concerns of making a movie are very complicated if you don't have the right connections. Even without fancy connections, you can successfully self-publish an audiobook in a reasonable amount of time.

3 Reality Checks:

1. It can get expensive.
Depending on which payment path you choose and how long your book turns out to be, an audiobook can set you back a few hundred to a few thousand dollars.

Industry standards change and each company has their own "standards" and structures. Last I checked, a deal needed to be $250 PFH to qualify as a SAG-AFTRA (Screen Actors Guild and the American Federation of Television and Radio Artists) contract. This is up from the $225 PFH it was a decade ago.

Most full novels range from about 8-11 hours of finished audio. Because I don't like math, let's use 10 hours. $250 x 10 hours = $2500. That's a pretty hefty bill if you intend to foot the whole thing all at once. I don't have to do the math to know that if you earn $4-5 for each audiobook sale that's going to require a heck of a lot of sales to break even.

2. These things take time and effort.

Individual narrator speed in cranking out your chapters depends on several factors, including what else is going on in their lives, how long your chapters are, and how quickly they can work. I am not a narrator but asking around has given me a few ballpark numbers to share with you. It takes about six hours of time to prepare one hour of finished audio. Pre-preparation can involve everything from reading the work, taking notes, and developing character voices. After that, the narrator must record the text, edit the chapter, and upload it to the distribution site.

My chapters tend to be around 2,000 words each, so typically, they're around 10-15 minutes of finished audio. Depending on the series, a book can be about 10,000, 50,000, or 90,000 words. My longest work in audio format is *Nadia's Tears*, which clocks in at ten hours and ten minutes. That is a 91,000-word story. *The Golden City Captives* came to 55 minutes, and that is about 10,000 words. Google tells me that the average 100,000-word book comes to 11 hours of finished audio. Let's go with a rough estimate of six hours to produce each finished hour. Doing the math, we get 66 hours. That's a lot of work. Keep in mind many narrators on ACX and Findaway Voices and other production companies have other jobs.

The narrator must:
- read your book
- come up with voices (you should have input in this part of the prep work) I recently learned that some narrators outsource the preproduction work too.
- record your book

- edit the files

Many narrators outsource the editing, which involves a cost. That's why most who have some experience do not accept straight Royalty Share deals anymore. They might be willing to donate their time in the hopes of making a profit later, but few are willing to incur debt to do it. Can't blame them for that. I'm sure they have bills to pay too.

After the files are uploaded, you (or somebody you hire) must review them. Whether you do this along the way or wait until the end, it still needs to be done. Then, the narrator makes the corrections and implements your suggestions. After you receive corrections, you should review it again. Next, it goes to the publishing company. From that point, it can take two to three weeks to go through their quality assurance checks and show up on retailers. (I've also heard of books that took three months to complete the quality assurance step.)

What affects the amount of time it takes to create an audiobook?
The timing depends on many variables. You should get a decent estimate from the formation of the contract. These details should be discussed before the contract's even offered.

Factors that can affect timing:
- **How much prep time the narrator needs** – This is affected by how difficult the subject matter is, the narrator's normal process, and the length of the manuscript. Fiction is not all created equal. Science fiction and fantasy tend to have more made up words than other genres. Pronunciation questions will significantly affect the difficulty of the project.
- **Whether the narrator does the editing themselves or outsources that part.** – The more people involved, the longer it will take if the files need to be emailed back and

forth. The exception is working with a studio. In my limited experience, studios tend toward a faster turnaround time.

- **The number of mistakes that need to be caught and corrected.** – It's like grading. Poor quality papers are always more time-consuming to grade than clean, error-free ones. The principle holds true for audiofiles.
- **Random things in your life or the narrator's life can impact the project.** – You might be able to power through a cold at your job, but anything that alters the narrator's voice will bring your production to a grinding halt. Family tragedies or sudden twists of fate can throw the routine out of whack for either of you.
- **How long ACX or your other distributor takes with quality control checks.** – There's not much you can do about this one. You're at the mercy of the publishing behemoths.

How much time are we talking about?

With that many variables, it's hard to give you an accurate estimate, so I'll simply share the timing of a recent project as a point of reference. I placed a few projects with a studio, which sped things up because the narrator went there to record and another professional handled the editing and mastering side of things.

From the moment of "Hey, I should make *Money Makes it Deadlier* an audiobook" to release, took about a month. It's only about 29,000 words, so if your book is a full-sized novel, you can expect it to take several months to complete. There was down time at the beginning and the end of the project. That's typical. The next few projects I completed with this studio were recorded in a week and reviewed in another, but quality control still tacked on about two weeks of wait time.

3. Audiobooks are not a "get rich quick" scheme.

Once you have a final product, you need to let people know it exists for it to sell. This requires yet more work and can be a slow process. It is possible to make money from audiobooks, just don't expect it to be overnight.

ACX recently revamped the way they do audiobook free codes. These are given to authors and narrators to help with getting reviews and gaining some traction. Royalties will no longer be paid for the free codes distributed for books published after March 26, 2020.

3 Answers to the Money Question: How much will this cost me?

The answer to that question varies widely, depending on how you choose to complete the project. The narrator likely wants to be paid. Since they're in for a lot of work, that's only fair. You're probably going to have to budget for this venture. It might help to define your goals. Are you in it for the art, the money, or some combination thereof?

The three basic answers to the money question:
- **The Free Path** – Royalty Share (RS)
- **The Paid Path** – Per Finished Hour (PFH)
- **The Hybrid Path** – a combination of RS and PFH or PFH and bonus payments, now officially RS$^+$ and Voices Share deals

Summary of the three paths:

Path Type	Financial Risk	Royalties
Royalty Share	Narrator	Split
Per Finished Hour	Author	Author
Royalty Share Plus	Shared	Split

Conclusion:

Audiobooks provide a wonderful way to present your story. The process takes a lot of work, but if you learn to enjoy the journey, I think you'll be happy with the results. You'll have a fabulous project you can be proud of and share with family, friends, and random strangers.

Chapter 3:
The Free Path

Introduction:

Some writers make a lot of money because they've built up the right fan base, but many struggle to sell enough to support the art, let alone make a living off of it. Still, there's no reason you should surrender dreams of hearing your story as an audiobook because of a tight budget.

What is Royalty Share (as applied to audiobooks)?

Royalty Share (RS) is a payment system available on ACX that can help you create an audiobook with relatively small financial risk. The narrator assumes the bulk of the risk for the project.

How does Royalty Share work?

Here's the general process:

1. The author posts their book for consideration, selecting "Royalty Share" in the payment options on ACX.
2. Narrators audition for the project.
3. The author selects a narrator.
4. The narrator produces the audiobook.
5. The author reviews the book.
6. The book is approved and goes through ACX's quality assurance sound checks before being released to the public.

With Royalty Share the current deal on ACX is a 50-50 split of 40% of the sale of each audiobook. So, you earn 20% of any audiobook sale once the title is released.

Random Rant: Yes, that means the company gets 60% of your blood, sweat, and tears for being an Amazon company and putting you in contact with your narrator. They also handle distribution, but in order to do a RS deal you must be exclusive to Audible. I believe a few years ago the percent that went to the author and narrator was higher. They used to "make up" for the appalling percentage by offering bonus payments, but that recently got revamped too. I believe you have referral links for your books. So, if somebody becomes an ACX subscriber through your advertising for the company, you earn a bounty. If you're good at doing free advertising for Amazon, you could make decent money this way, but that's a lot of hustle work.

Caution: Audiobooks can be difficult to sell. Not every reader likes listening to somebody else read them the story. Some people don't even know audiobooks exist. Having more outlets for your stories is great, but don't count on it to get you out of debt immediately.

Sharing is part of the deal:
I've heard rumors of authors balking at doing Royalty Share projects because they don't want to split the profits. That's the deal though. The narrator invests their time and talents to create the audiobook with the assumption that sales eventually lead to a profit. They may have other reasons of wishing to work with you. Perhaps they're a fan who wants to help you realize your hopes and dreams of a fabulous audiobook. They could want to keep their skills sharp by working your project in between ones that pay their bills. Whatever the reason, people tend not to give random strangers a gift worth $2000 or more without the hope of some return.

Advantages for the author:

- Free is always good. As mentioned previously, the narrator takes on the bulk of the financial risks.
- You have a better chance of discovering a budding narrator starting on their journey.
- You get to hear how another artist interprets what you've written.
- The narrator gets a cut of each sale, so he or she is very invested in the title's success.
- If this is one of the early titles for the narrator, they may be more willing to help with promotions. Don't expect them to put up money, but they might answer interview questions and be proactive about sending out their promotion codes to family and friends.

Disadvantages for the author:

- You must be exclusive to Audible. It's one of the biggest companies but not the only distributor out there.
- You're at the mercy of the narrator's schedule. Often, the narrators do this as a side gig because they love it. If they need to hold down a regular job to pay their bills, it's likely going to take longer to produce your book.
- Since you're not paying the narrator, you should be more cognizant of how nitpicky you get with your comments and directions to them.

Advantages for the narrator:

- Discover a new author to love.
- Work at your own pace. Since you're assuming the financial risk, you have a greater measure of control over what happens and when it happens.
- The more titles you turn out, the more money you'll make. In time, you could potentially have hundreds of titles to your credit. It's a numbers game. If you have more authors promoting their books narrated by you, there's a greater chance listeners will fall in love with your voice and

purchase other books.

Disadvantages for the narrator:
- You're taking on most of the financial risk. You probably know better than I do how much time, effort, and creativity it takes to turn written words into memorable performances.
- The book must stay with Audible.

Side note:
Never lie to the narrator. If you can't afford to pay somebody to voice your book, that's fine, but be honest about it. Don't put your book up as a $100 PFH project or RS when you know that all you can afford is the RS. It's shady, and nobody likes shady.

Hidden costs:
Although the narrator may help with promoting an audiobook, the responsibility—and cost—falls to the author. Remember, if people do not know it exists, they won't buy it. The ad costs are reasonable, but even $10 here and there can add up.

Consider offering a gift or a bonus:
The nature of gift giving and receiving can be tricky, and a surprising number of people have very little common sense about stuff like this.

Gift vs. bonus:
- A gift is likely a one-time thing. The gift should be delivered after the book completes as a thank you for the many hours of love and labor put into transforming your book into an audiobook. The gift doesn't necessarily have to be monetary, though it could be. It can also take the form of gift cards or other tokens of appreciation.
- A bonus can be delivered in increments as the audiobook is forming or all at once after it's released. The difference

is that a gift would likely be a surprise while a bonus is something you'd probably mention beforehand.

GIFT VS BONUS

How is this different than the hybrid way?
It will differ from the hybrid way in terms of amount. A gift or bonus is a gesture of appreciation offered, not something expected or contracted.

Be a supportive partner to the narrator:
This concept should prevail regardless of which payment path you choose, but it's especially vital for the Royalty Share method because you're not contracted to pay a set amount of money. It's likely a gross oversimplification to say something like pay them in praise and gratitude, but there's some truth to the sentiment.

Ever done something nice for somebody else that took a lot of time and effort, then had them ignore or disdain the gesture? It's even worse to have the person you're doing the nice thing for nitpick everything about your efforts and then tell you to hurry up. Making an audiobook takes time and effort. Yes, it's the job they signed up for, but showing you acknowledge and appreciate their time and talents will go a long way in fostering a strong relationship with them.

Conclusion:

"I can't afford that" simply isn't true when it comes to commissioning the creation of an audiobook. Royalty Share opens the way for thousands of titles that wouldn't normally be released in this format. That's awesome, but it also ups the amount of competition you have. So, make sure your story's unforgettable.

Chapter 4:
The Paid Path

Introduction:

Creating audiobooks costs time and money. The amount of time and money depends on several factors, but if you're like me and must hire the services of a narrator, the money amount goes up and the time amount goes down. One of my friends narrates her own mystery books. They turn out pretty well, but aside from lacking that skill, I enjoy working with other artists.

What is Per Finished Hour?

PFH is where you agree to pay a set amount per finished audiobook hour. This is different than an hour's worth of work on the book because it typically takes about six hours to prep one finished audiobook hour. Narrators have different ways of estimating the time it takes, but this includes reading the manuscript, creating voices, recording the performance, and editing the file afterwards. Some narrators outsource the editing part. Outsourcing incurs costs.

What goes into a finished hour?

I once saw a beautiful graphic on this, but I didn't agree with every single part. I'm also not a narrator, so I'm going to keep this at the level of my knowledge. In order to deliver a finished product, the narrator needs to read over the story and take some voice notes on the manuscript. Next, they need to perform the story. After that, the files need to be edited to take out the random noises, fix word mispronunciations, and remove breaths that slip into the recording. The files also need to be proofed, though you can and should take on that role. The narrator needs to implement any changes or edit out any mistakes caught during the proofing stage. The files also need to be uploaded to ACX or another audiobook distributor.

Why should the author proof the files?

This is your story. You know the plot and characters best. Sometimes, the narrator chooses to interpret the words differently than you've intended. I'm not saying to micromanage the narrator, but if there's a line or two delivered with unintended inflection, feel free to point it out.

Before the rough copy is uploaded, I'm sure it's already gone through an extensive amount of editing. Still, strange noises can occur. It's best to have multiple ears on a project.

This is the fun part. Presumably, you're hiring somebody to make you an audiobook because you want to know what your story sounds like when it's brought to life by a professional voice actor.

Additional bonus:
Having stuff read aloud by a professional can also point out mistakes that somehow made it through your personal rounds of edits, beta readers, and the many flavors of editors you already hired. Please understand that I am not saying you should rely on this as a substitution for editing. It is not the narrator's responsibility to be your content or line editor. That said, if a mistake is found, fix it.

PFH rates vary widely:

I've seen as low as $35 PFH all the way up to $500 PFH. I'm at the point in my life and career where $150-$200 PFH per project is feasible. Please note that this is on the low end of the scale.

From lurking in some narrator groups, I've learned many consider anything less than $150-$200 PFH insulting. Industry standard is indeed $250 PFH. I hear many stories of people getting offered $35 PFH. Even for a short book, that's about $6 per hour of work. If this is the maximum you can afford than I highly recommend a hybrid deal. Something this small could cover outsourced editing but not much more. If you really believe your project has potential, continue to seek ways to turn it into an audiobook.

Why would anybody agree to a ridiculously low PFH?
You may find somebody willing to work for a crazy low PFH. The chances of them being brand new to the business are high. If they've never done this before, they may not be aware of the tremendous work involved in making the audiobook.

Julie C. Gilbert

Advantages for the author:

- You don't have to share once the project completes. You will earn full royalties for each book sold.
- You can discuss with your narrator when and how things are paid.
  Note: This does not hold true if you've chosen a contract that will be SAG-AFTRA. Those need to have payment sent all at once in the end by check to a separate company, not the narrator. The union takes their cut and then pays the narrator the difference.
- You will certainly have interest in your book regardless of sales. A book's rank and performance matters a lot more for Royalty Share pitches. You can skip all that if you're offering a PFH rate.
- You have a wider range of narrators to choose from. These often come with more experience. Many narrators only audition for PFH projects regularly. They may be willing to do Royalty Share under special circumstances, but that's rare.
- The transaction is more straightforward. You are a customer hiring a professional to do a job. Most narrators want you to be satisfied with the product. Under the principle of you get what you pay for, you have more of a right to corrections and quality control.
  Note: This is not a license to arbitrarily scrap ten finished hours of audiobook because you don't like it, then refuse to pay the narrator upon completion. If you want a main character to sound a certain way, say so from the start. That's what the 15-minute check exists for.
  Second note: Not every side character with a line of dialogue needs a distinct voice.

Disadvantages for the author:

- You might have to wade through a lot of mediocre and bad auditions. PFH jobs are sort of the dream. Everybody trying to get into the business will audition if you offer a

28

competitive PFH. It will be tempting to send a contract to the first voice you love but take your time with the decision.

- The narrator you choose may have an extensive backlog of titles. Even if they want to help you promote the book, the demands on their time tends to be greater.
- The narrator receives their last payday for the project before it goes to quality control for final distribution. Most want the title to do well, but since they do not receive part of the royalties, they are not externally motivated to pound the pavement to generate sales.
- The financial burden for the project rests solely on you. Those finished hours can add up quickly if you've offered a fair PFH.

Advantages for the narrator:

- You get paid! There's little to no financial risk to a PFH project. If there is a financial risk, you should know it right away since this is still the most straightforward of the money paths.
  Note: I recommend asking for progress payments. I've heard enough horror stories of people being stiffed on long projects. Also, keep in mind that these things can take months to complete.
- You can be more productive. Concentrate on the craft and outsource the boring parts. I still say the author or rights holder should be heavily invested in the proofing portion of the venture, but from what I can gather, the time-consuming piece is editing. Outsourcing the editing portion can lead to an overall cleaner product. Also, you can pick up more projects instead of spending your time cleaning up the audiofiles.
- The author may be heavily involved in the creative process. This can be a good thing. The author should be able to give you detailed voice notes that will help you with the preparation portions. He or she should also be able to answer your questions about the book.

Disadvantages for the narrator:

- You stop getting paid before the project finishes.
- The author may be heavily involved in the creative process. You'll note that this is both an advantage and a disadvantage based on the author who hired you. Some people are nuts. I've heard of people sending narrators over fifty pages of voice notes. Even if that's hyperbole, I can see such a thing happening.
- You might be micromanaged. There is a higher chance of the author being a demanding diva. Some people have unrealistic expectations and lack the education in the business to recognize this. You might not realize that your job included polite author education, but many jobs come with unexpected additional roles. (I'm a high school teacher. Translation: I get to temporarily be mom, counselor, judge, cheerleader, nurse, exterminator, janitor, and referee. On certain special days, I get to do all those roles in the same period.)
- You might have the opposite problem: little to no direction from the author (then yelling when you fail to meet the expectations that existed only in his or her head). The rights holder can make the assumption that if you're the professional hired to complete the project, you should be handling everything.

The reason PFH contracts can get emotionally tricky.

There's a natural human tendency to believe that money spent affords the right to better service. Furthermore, there's confusion about what "better service" entails. The concept's simple enough. It's: you get what you pay for. It's similar to when parents of private school students make irrational assumptions about their child's grade potential. The unwritten assumption is that the money spent on tuition should be able to purchase the best education possible. Translation: they think "best education" means instant A's all around. Even those offering $35 PFH abide by that concept. In fact, I'd venture to say that these people are more likely to be demanding.

As if the issue wasn't muddled enough, they're not completely wrong. Narrators are independent contractors who have offered a service for a price. On the surface, details should be clear. The narrator agrees to deliver an audiobook of approximately X number of hours for Y amount of money per finished hour. The complications kick in when authors and narrators have different expectations on how things sound, when files are uploaded, and how clean the audiofiles must be.

Conclusion:

Contracts where the author or rights holder pays a set amount per finished hour of audiobook can be the most straightforward, but as with anything, money complicates the matter. Some people mistake offering a PFH rate as purchasing a license to make as many demands as they desire.

Chapter 5:
The Hybrid Path

Introduction:

Back when I started having my books made into audiobooks, there was no official way to do hybrid projects. They were worked out directly between author and narrator. I continue to do most of my hybrid projects on the unofficial path due to my financial situation. In short, I have a day job that allows me to commission audiobooks. That said, I still find parting with a few thousand dollars at one time painful, so I prefer progress payments.

What is the hybrid path?

A "hybrid deal" typically refers to a Royalty Share deal where you also agree to pay the narrator an additional amount of money. Early projects worked out as RS plus bonuses, but these days, my hybrid path is probably better defined as PFH plus bonuses.

ACX has recently legitimized the path by making Royalty Share Plus a real thing. Eventually, I'd like to try one of these projects, but I've not done one yet. While there's much speculation about what this method entails, I believe it's a RS project that also comes with an additional PFH payment to the narrator. The difference is that the PFH rate is way lower than it would normally be.

How does the hybrid path work?

From ACX's blog announcement, I gather it's run like a RS deal on the back end and a PFH deal on the front end. By that, I mean that like a normal PFH deal, the narrator will have to click a button that says they received their fee before the book goes to quality assurance. After the audiobook releases, ACX will do the RS calculations automatically as sales happen.

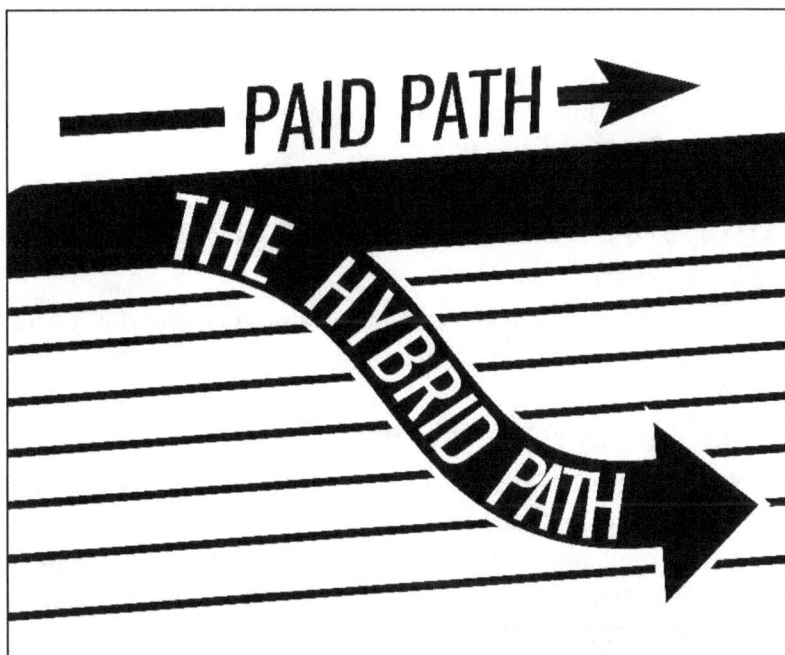

Advantages for authors:

- It still minimizes the upfront cost of creating an audiobook.
- It's more attractive to narrators and will get you more auditions because there's less financial risk for them.
- You're supporting another professional in the creation of something grand.
- The narrator is heavily invested in the book's success because the size of their payday is tied directly to the audiobook's fate.

- Building relationships is important. Even if you can't afford to pay the industry standard for an audiobook, the narrator will appreciate whatever investment you're capable of making.

Relationship aside: Gifts are good for building a relationship. If you can't afford any sort of regular payments to your narrator, consider giving them a gift card or some other one-time gift to let them know you appreciate the work they do. Money paid for a job is not a gift, but anything you can do above and beyond can be. Good communication makes these author-narrator relationships work best, so the more you can learn about the narrator, the smoother future projects will run.

Always be honest and clear in your audition description:
If you're willing to consider RS$^+$, mention that. But don't bring it up solely to get more auditions.

Disadvantages for authors:
- You get less per book sale because you've agreed to split royalties with the narrator.
- It could take quite a while to earn back the investment. You also need to be aware that you may never earn your investment back.
- There could still be time delays. Narrators often set up multiple projects at once. If your project doesn't pay as much as others they've arranged, you may find it gets a lower priority. That's human nature. They will likely still abide by the contract to the best of their ability, but if you're asking for the 4th round of alterations, don't be surprised if there are delays.

Advantages for narrators:

- There's less financial risk for you. This isn't an instant fix, and you are still assuming much of the risk involved in the project. However, the additional payment makes it more likely you won't lose money in the process, only time.
- There's the chance that the manuscript has gone through some quality controls before it reaches you. If people are willing to invest something in their project's audiobook, they have likely invested in other things that lead to a better book. Proofreading, covers, editing, and advertising also cost money.
  Warning: This is not foolproof! Plenty of people have more money than sense to use it well. Your best bet is to look the book up on Amazon and read a few pages of it.
- The author is probably going to be heavily invested in the project's success. Nobody's looking for their plan to fail, but if the author is willing to pay something, they are more likely to help you any way they can. That could be a delusion on my part, but I'd like to believe it's a fair assumption.
- The author may be new to making audiobooks. The upside is you may have a chance at molding how they think of the process.
- You can build a relationship with the author.

Disadvantages for narrators:

- You're still gambling on the idea that the audiobook sales will make your labor investment pay off later.
- The author may be new to making audiobooks. This can be good and bad. The downside comes in the higher chance for unrealistic expectations.
- There's the potential for the author to have a sense of entitlement without investing much monetarily.

Unique challenges to hybrid systems:

- In an official capacity, these types of deals are brand new and very much misunderstood. Willfully or not, many authors have no idea that RS$^+$ means they contractually agree to pay the narrator something.
- People abuse the system by claiming they'll do an RS$^+$ contract without the intent of follow through. It's wrong, and they probably even know it's wrong. It'll happen anyway.

My hybrid system before they were officially a thing:

I've always tried to be fair to my narrators. In the past, whether the project was PFH or RS, I made payments until the rate came to about $225 a finished hour. This often took months, so it didn't seem like a couple of thousand dollars. The catch was that the narrator had to trust me to send payments according to my open-ended timeframe. The PFH rate in the contract might have been as low as $50, but in recent years, I've bumped that up to $100. The only difference is how much must be paid before the project goes to quality control.

I'm aware that not everybody's financial situation lets them do this, which is why things like RS$^+$ exist. These days, I'm more apt to offer a flat $200 PFH contract if the book is short enough. If it's long, I'll have to consider other options because I simply can't afford that much of an investment all at once.

Note: My rates are middle range. They are by no means the most generous that exist. However, they are strong enough to grab the interest of a wide range of professionals.

Why would I do this when I could get the audiobooks created for free?

To understand my logic, you're going to have to listen to a soap-box speech. Writing may be a business, but it's also a passion, a joy, and an art. Stories are meant to be shared, and getting stories into as many formats as possible helps reach the widest amount of people. It's the same logic as why I bothered formatting a large print version of some of my stories.

I love working with narrators to develop the characters and breathe a new kind of life into a story. In addition to a general admiration for what narrators do, I believe in the principle of paying workers for their labors.

I'm aware that people have varying definitions of fairness. Some would say that even $100 PFH isn't worth the time or effort the narrators put in, and they're 100% entitled to this opinion. They have a right to forego auditioning for my projects. It's probably for the best anyway. A relationship wherein one party already feels cheated by the other is likely doomed.

Why I personally haven't run RS$^+$ projects yet:

Since my philosophy typically doesn't allow for me to run a project at less than $200 PFH eventually, it doesn't make sense for me to do a royalty split if I can afford the outright cost. If I find a very long project with good commercial potential, I may try RS$^+$ someday. Audiobooks are one of the expanding fields of the book industry. I just haven't worked up to trying it yet.

Conclusion:

Hybrid projects offer a nice middle ground and third option for those looking to have their books made into audiobooks. I've instinctively done them from the beginning, but it's nice to know that they are official now.

Chapter 6:
Overview of My Audiobook Process

Introduction:

Before jumping into the breakdown of individual steps, I want to let you see the short version of the process as it unfolds because it's easy to lose that big picture when studying details.

Note: The layout is geared for working with ACX. Findaway Voices will do most of the narrator selection process for you.

Decide which book to turn into an audiobook:

The simple version of audiobook economics are as follows. If you pay a narrator to create the audiobook for you, it can get very expensive. That would favor the creation of smaller projects. However, most audiobooks are sold on websites with a credit system. Subscribers buy credits to spend on audiobooks of any length. This favors the creation of longer projects.

Why is length a factor in a credit system?

In short, people want to get the most for their money. If they have a choice between spending a credit on a two-hour book or a twelve-hour book, they will likely jump on the longer book because it offers more hours of entertainment for the price.

Credit System and Length Factor:

People will lean towards longer books in order to get more for their money.

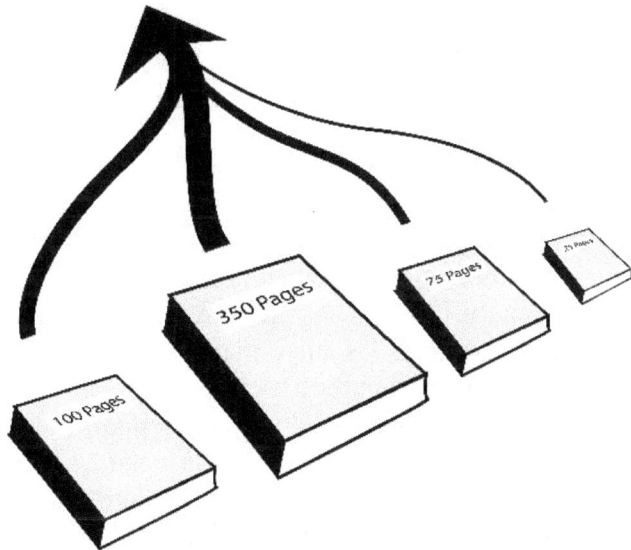

The advantage of short series:
When possible, try to turn a series of shorter books into audiobooks. The first will typically sell the best, but if you own the rights to the whole series, you have the option of creating a combination audiobook. Combos are attractive to the credit spenders for the reason listed above. I'm currently testing this theory with the Shadow Council series. Each individual story is about 3.5 hours long, so the combo should be roughly 14 hours. I can't report on its success yet as the whole series has not released yet, but if you keep in touch through social media, I would be happy to share whether or not the experiment performs as planned.

Economics of a short book at $200 PFH:
Remember, I like easy math. Let's say a book comes to three finished hours. This will set me back $600. It happens that the people working on the Shadow Council series can do roughly half the book each recording day. I send $200 when the first half posts, $200 when the second half posts, and anything left as I approve the final book.

Why I like progress payments:
In the interest of transparency, I'll let you know that thus far, I've spent more money on audiobooks than I've made. I can afford to do this because I have a day job. Progress payments allow me to spread out the cost. Usually, that's enough time for my bank account to recover from the shock. (Kidding. Mostly. Never stress your bank account over creating an audiobook. A lot of the choices I've made increase the cost, but you need to work within your budget.) Audiobooks are an investment that will generate income over time. How much depends on factors like quality and subject matter.

Choose the type of narrator I'm looking for:
Nonfiction books can go either way in terms of which "voice" would be more appropriate. There are probably dozens of things you should consider when selecting a narrator for your project. I'm going to cover the most important of these.

Factors I consider when choosing a narrator:
- Budget
- Character details
- Personal preference
- Number of characters
- Subject matter (especially in nonfiction)
- Narrator ability vs. number of characters
- Narrator availability and the project timeline

Side note: I'll include an annotated version of this list in chapter 9.

New narrators vs. seasoned narrators:
Those still learning the business may be more willing to work with lower budgets. Among these, you'll find a wealth of talented people, rough diamonds, and those who probably shouldn't give up their day job … ever.

Those with more experience can command a higher PFH rate and become far choosier about which kinds of RS or RS$^+$ projects they accept. They may be beyond your budget, but to a certain extent it's true that you get what you pay for.

You probably wouldn't hire a plumber to replace your entire piping system if he or she had no experience. You'd expect the plumber candidate to have gone through an extensive training program, complete with a lot of hands-on practice. In that analogy, if your house is part of the plumber-to-be's training process, you hope he or she has a good mentor double checking the work. For better or worse, there's no set standardized school for becoming a narrator. Like any other profession, they learn by doing. The first jobs done are good but later ones tend to be better as the narrator's skills sharpen.

Male vs. female voices:
Personal preference, narration point of view, and subject matter kick in here. I mentioned hiring a man because I loved his voice. He backed out because the book itself was completely first-person narration from the point of view of two teenage girls. The change in perspective never even occurred to me, but he was absolutely right. While men can do credible female voices and women can do credible male voices, the closer the main protagonist can be to the narrator's natural voice, the easier the project will be for him or her.

When in doubt, I open auditions for both male and female narrators. There's nothing wrong with not knowing right away which kind of voice will fit. Many books have large sections that feature both male and female characters. Typically, I make the choice based off of the main character's gender.

It may even be necessary to hire two narrators to bring your vision to life. I have never had to do this, but I have listened to several projects that feature two narrators.

Note: If you are commissioning two narrators, the project should be PFH. RS is messy enough with two people, let alone three.

Select an audition script (or two) and upload it to ACX:

Choosing a great audition script involves more than slapping up chapter 1. I consider the excerpt's length and difficulty. Ideally, I'm looking for something around 500-1,000 words that shows the main character(s), a few side characters, and some normal narration sections. The narrator who gets the job will need to be able to handle each of these things and more.

Criteria for a great audition script:
- Around 500-1,000 words
- Includes the main character
- Includes a few side characters
- Includes some normal narration sections

Listen to audio samples and send invitations:

Samples and invites go hand-in-hand.

Have you ever loved or hated a voice instantly? Some people possess awesome voices, but what appeals to listeners can vary. Sometimes, I love a person's voice, but they're not right for the story. They naturally sound too old or young or perky for the part. I can typically tell within ten to thirty seconds if I would hire somebody based off their voice quality or the skill of the samples they've uploaded to ACX. Some people have excellent voices, but their samples have a lot of static or sound like they're speaking through a tin can.

I prepare a general invitation that outlines the project, the terms, the audition window, and a link to where they can find the project. Sending invitations can be tedious, but it's usually worth the time investment. When I find an enjoyable sample, I send the person the invitation to audition. Sometimes, I try to modify the form letter to be a little more personal, but this is a business and most people understand the necessity of a form letter.

As I send audition invitations, I prepare a list of the 10-15 people I would consider hiring for the project. The list simply says the person's name and what they're willing to work for. Most of the ones I'm interested in are the $100-200 PFH range, but I also look at $200-400 PFH range people as well.

Listen to auditions and select a narrator:

Getting that first audition feels amazing. Getting the thirtieth feels less amazing. Several auditions are rejected outright because of voice mismatch or poor audio quality, but often, I get two to three very strong candidates. Then, comes the hard part: I can only hire one narrator.

How do I break a tie?

Sometimes, I message both top candidates to discuss terms because that can be a tiebreaker. Often, this step makes me feel lousier when I have to tell the runner-up that somebody else got the job.

Now that I've done this a few times, I've made some friends in the business. Occasionally, I'll send the top auditions to these trusted individuals for their opinion.

The most common method of tiebreaking is listening to the top auditions on repeat. I'll be listening to the narrator a lot, so it follows that I should be able to still enjoy the audition after a few rounds of hearing it in a row.

Message everybody who auditioned:
Great communication matters in every sphere of life.

I prepare several form letters then move through the list of auditioners and place their name by the letter they receive after the message goes through. Whether it's two or twenty messages, I take the time to send thank you emails informing them that the project has been placed.

Message the winner, discuss terms in detail, and send the contract:
At this point, I get the top candidate's email and stop using ACX's clunky messaging system. Usually, I ask the narrator what they want the contract to say. This varies per person. Some people dictate terms very close to their working speed, while others build in some extra "life-happens" time.

Setting up the contract only takes a few minutes because by this point there should be no questions or concerns or surprises in what it'll say.

Deliver the manuscript and voice notes:
Sending the manuscript is a matter of composing a short email.

Creating the voice notes takes more time, but it's kind of fun. I haven't read some of these stories in ages. It's nice to revisit while reacquainting myself with the characters.

Review the audiobook files:
I usually end up listening to every file at least three times. The first round is as the files come in. I read along with the manuscript. Sometimes, I listen again without the manuscript while doing something mundane like formatting a book for paperback. That listen is to see the general entertainment value of the story being delivered. It's critical that the first review take place as soon as possible to the files being uploaded and early in the overall

recording process because it's the time to fix pacing issues, character voice concerns, and critical word pronunciations. The second official round or file review is after receiving corrections. The third round comes before sending the final payment and approving the book for publication.

For each round, I offer color coded notes for each chapter uploaded. You don't have to use colors, but it does make it prettier. I use purple for things I love, dark green for general comments, light blue for explanatory comments, orange for possible mistakes, and red for things that are definite mistakes.

Receive corrections and conduct a final project review:
Even if I'm not going to recheck a file from start to finish, I'll spot check the places I'd pointed out mistakes or any other requested changes. Afterwards, I listen once more beginning to end. The final review can be with or without the manuscript, but it should be a little more intense than casually listening for sheer enjoyment. A poorly done audiobook can harm a book's reputation. If you write a lot of books, I'm sure you'll want people to check out other titles, so having a clean, error free audiobook is important.

Send final payment if PFH and hit approve:
Payment details should be discussed at length with your narrator before they begin working on the project. I prefer to send the PFH rate for each hour of audiofiles that get posted. Then, the final payment goes out after my last round of reviews as I'm approving the project to go to ACX's quality control minions.

Conclusion:
A few of these steps could be skipped but do so at your own risk. The more involved you are in the endeavor, the higher chance you have of having the final product meet your expectations. I'm also told that being involved is reassuring to narrators. Having two sets of ears track mistakes can save in terms of stress levels (for you and the narrator) as well as ease production time.

Chapter 7:
Step #1: Selecting a Path … and a Book

Introduction:

Choosing whether to do Royalty Share, PFH, or RS$^+$ might seem like an easy thing to do because it's largely based on facts that aren't going to change quickly. You need to pick the one that's right for you. Likewise, you may need to choose an appropriate book to begin with. The following are some thoughts to guide you through both major decisions.

Questions to ask yourself before commissioning the creation of an audiobook:

Several questions may not favor one path over another, but each one needs to be answered at some point.

Why do I want my book to be an audiobook?

- **I want to hear my book performed** – This could go either way. I will reiterate that PFH jobs get more auditions overall, but only enter that arena if you can legitimately afford it. If you can pay some now and some later, then work out a private deal with the prospective narrator. On the other hand, RS offers a low-risk option for you.

- **I want to make money** – The right answer for you will depend heavily on your sales. If you can reasonably expect strong audiobook sales, you are better off fronting the money PFH style and reaping the full benefits of the royalties. If audiobook sales may not be that strong, you're better off with one of the RS systems.

What can I afford to invest in the audiobook's creation?

- **Little to nothing** – That makes this an easy decision. Go RS.
- **Something but certainly not a few hundred to a few thousand dollars** – RS$^+$ looks like a promising option for you. It involves some initial monetary input, but probably won't immediately murder your bank account.
- **Money's not a problem** – PFH is the logical choice for you.

How much financial risk can I afford right now?

You might think this is the same question as the previous one. However, there's a subtle but powerful difference in immediacy. PFH jobs can add up very quickly. RS$^+$ offers lesser rewards but also involves less financial risk. RS is the least financially risky but also tends to be the most limiting in terms of the willing narrator pool.

Don't be afraid to make your own path:

Do the math for your project before making any promises you might not be able to keep. I prefer PFH or my own hybrid options. A hybrid path of my own choosing gives me the time to spread out the payments yet allows me to ultimately get the narrator a decent wage in the end.

How long is the book I'm looking to turn into an audiobook?

How well word count translates to audiobook minutes depends on the nature of the section. The average is about 9,300 words to an hour of audiobook. Length will factor heavily into your choice about which payment path to pursue because it determines the overall project cost. Short stories and novellas are easier to justify PFH costs because they don't amount to as much as longer projects. A 75,000-word novel is easily going to push the 8-hour mark. Even at $200 PFH, that can cost a bundle very quickly.

If all you write is epic fantasy that always clocks in well over the 100K mark, cost might prohibit you from doing PFH. That's why the other paths exist. It might be harder for you to catch the interest of a narrator, but that doesn't immediately translate to impossible.

How complicated is this book going to be for somebody to read aloud?

If your book involves a lot of different voices that must be distinct, you will require an actor or actress with a higher degree of skill. If your book is nonfiction with only one voice and little to no dialogue, you need a different skillset. The ability to realistically portray multiple voices is less important, but the ability to choose natural, realistic, and engaging points of inflection may become more vital. Regardless of the kind of skill you're seeking, having more money to invest tends to open more doors of opportunity.

Do I really have to choose a path?

Technically, you can present your project as RS, RS⁺, and a PFH range. I believe I've done this before because I truly had not made up my mind yet as to the best path for me. However, my time among some narrator-heavy social groups tells me that this is an easy way to drive off some interest. Enough people have pulled this as a trick that narrators are wary. Expect some pointed questions. If you can explain yourself well in the description, you should be fine if you're not set on a path.

Benefits of choosing a path:

- It sets a precedent of clear communication.
- People think you know your mind. That might be an illusion, but it's a nice one.
- Those interested in that method of payment can audition. Others can move on with a clear conscience.
- As discussed previously, offering competitive PFH rates can be very attractive to narrators and result in a higher number of auditions. If you can only do RS or RS$^+$, that's fine. Talk up the book other ways. What makes you think it has the potential to sell well in audio format?

How to choose the right book:

Having only one book makes this an easy decision, but since most authors aren't one-hit wonders, you likely have a choice.

The factors that affect this decision will influence the skillset required in the narrator you seek. When you have the choice, you may wish to pick the "easier" option for your first project. There will be enough learning curves along the way.

Factors to consider:

- **Length** – Short is easier to make. Long tends to be easier to sell because people feel like they get more for their credit. There are no right or wrong answers here, only a difference in expected results and challenges you will face along the way.
- **Genre** – As with selling ebooks or paperbacks, genre factors in heavily to sales. Romance and clean romance have very strong presences in the audiobook world, as does mystery. It's good because that means there's a lot of interest in those genres. It's bad in that it also means you will have some stiff competition when it comes to catching the listener's attention.
- **Number of distinct voices** – Most books have a ton of characters, but the difference is how many do you expect to come across as distinct voices? If you absolutely must have eight distinct voices, you need to hire somebody with that ability. That's probably going to cost you more and limit the pool of viable candidates.
- **Accents and made up languages** – If you have a contemporary book with no unusual words and an epic science fiction novel, you may want to start out with the simpler one. If you choose to tackle the one with strange accents and languages, provide the narrator with detailed notes.

  Side note: Try not to go overboard. General American is one of the accent choices on ACX. If your story has a distinct need like 1840's rural Georgia, you should probably mention that. If the project calls for over a dozen distinct regional accents, you should be upfront about it right on the audition page. You'll probably still find somebody up to the challenge, but you do not want them walking into that project blind. They'll be displeased. You'll be disappointed. It could get ugly.
- **Timeframe** – Best not to be in a hurry. Shorter books naturally can be completed quicker than longer projects, but you should always assume deadlines are fluid.

I've chosen a path and a book ... now what?

Congratulations. You've taken your first step into a wider world. If you're going with a company besides ACX, the next few steps might vary, but the concept's going to be similar.

The what now step-by-step style:
- **Claim your book** – Sign into ACX with the same credentials you get into your Amazon account. If you have a separate one solely for your business, then be sure to use that one. They might change the placement, but currently there's an "Add Your Title" link in the top right corner of the webpage. Type your title into the search bar and claim the book. If you have a common title, then type that in plus your name or the pen name you used to write the book.
- **Continue the title setup** – This involves everything from reading—or at least saying you read—the agreement to answering a bunch of questions about the book, the copyright, the type (fiction vs. nonfiction), the category (genre), whether you want auditions or not, describing your dream narrator, anything else you can say to sell it to narrators, and uploading an audition script.
- **Answer more nosy project questions** – The next set of questions has more to do with money than anything else. This is where you declare the path you've chosen. It's click boxes, so you can choose multiple ones, but if you do click more than one, you should explain in the previous notes section.
- **Wait for the auditions to roll in** – I'll discuss these in more details in the next two chapters, but I recommend leaving an audition window of at least a week. This information should be readily available to those auditioning for the book.

What kinds of instructions and details should be in the audition notes?

Anything that truthfully presents your book in a better light. ACX mentions things like a strong social media presence, stellar book sales, any marketing plans, and so forth.

Things I recommend including in the audition notes:

- **The deal** – If it's a RS$^+$ or a PFH offering, you should include exactly what you mean by that. You can put in a small range of numbers, but gigantic ranges are useless. You want to do everything in your power to help the narrator decide whether to spend the effort auditioning or move on to another project. $35 PFH and $200 PFH have different levels of attractive power.
- **Book length** – Sometimes, narrators are looking for a certain length project.
- **Series potential** – You don't need to mention if it's standalone unless you want to, but it might be more attractive if you can safely say you intend to take the whole series to audiobook.
- **Marketing Plan** – Numbers always help, but this is especially important for RS and RS$^+$ type jobs.
- **Content warnings** – Strong language, sensitive topics, extreme violence, and explicit sex scenes are some of the many types of content warnings you should consider including. It will attract some narrators and repel others. This is good because it avoids wasting people's time, including your own.
- **Short character notes** – I purposefully keep these vague because part of my evaluation of auditions involves the narrator's interpretation of the characters presented in the text. At this point, I want to see how well their reading instincts line up with my own.
- **Timeframe for auditions** – I still recommend at least a week, especially if you are inviting narrators to audition, but I usually add a disclaimer that they should message me

if it's nearing the end of that timeframe. I'd hate for somebody to be ready to upload an audition only to find it already placed with another narrator.

- **The scene if it's not readily apparent from the description** – If the excerpt doesn't set the scene, you may wish to give some background details.

Conclusion:

Although tempting to gloss over this step altogether, every decision made here is foundational. How you choose to pay can change the dynamics of the relationship you have with the narrator. The type of book you select can vastly alter the sort of narrator you need.

Chapter 8:
Step #2: Audition Script Selection and Narrator Homework

Introduction:

After choosing to hire somebody to turn your book into an audiobook, you'll need to select an audition script and decide which kind of narrator to seek. Narrators come in many flavors and vintages. Pairing the right narrator to the perfect project is an art form you'll learn to love if you continue commissioning audiobooks. Unless you know an awesome narrator because he or she is your neighbor, you'll have to find one the old-fashioned way: through good research and hard work.

What do you want your audition script to do?

Ideally, the audition script should give you a chance to test a narrator's abilities and range. Depending on the book's complexity, you'll need to know if the narrator candidate can handle the accents, unique character voices, languages, and descriptions.

What makes an awesome audition script?

- **Around 500-1,000 words** – The average number of words that will make a finished hour of audiobook is around 9,300. This comes to about three and a half minutes on the short end and seven minutes on the long end. As exciting as getting auditions can be, remember you must listen to each of them. If you end up with thirty auditions, that's a very long time. Also, understand that you're asking people to invest time and effort when they audition.

Note: The shorter you can get the audition script the better. Even a 5-minute script is asking the narrators to do a half-hour's worth of work.

- **Features the main character** – If you have more than one main character, try to find something that contains both. As with any acting application, you need to know if the main characters have great chemistry. If you're one of those rare people who can afford to hire both a male and a female narrator, then you should open auditions to both genders and offer selections for each.

- **Captures the voice of the story** – If your book is mostly lighthearted, don't choose the darkest passage for the audition script. You're better served by choosing something more representative of the whole thing.

- **Mixes dialogue and description** – You will need to know how the narrator handles both types of passages.
  Side note: I once had a man audition whose rolling cadence nearly made me seasick. He has gotten other jobs, but we would not have been a good match by any stretch.

- **Features at least some side characters** – Although less important, it's nice to get a feel for how the narrator approaches side character voices.

AWESOME

500-1000 Words

Features the main character

Captures the voice of the story

Features some side characters

Mixes dialogue and description

AUDITION SCRIPT

Longer isn't necessarily better:
If you select something too long, you might scare off potential candidates. The more seasoned ones will only do part of the audition script if it's too long. I have given the job to people who didn't complete the script for one reason or another.

You'll have to listen to this passage many times if you get a lot of great auditions.

Consider picking two passages:
If you do this, be clear that the narrators should pick one or pieces from both. You should not require them to do both passages, unless they are very short. The total word count should still be somewhere less than 1,000 words. I have done longer, but there's no distinct advantage to having a longer audition set. This might be especially important if your book features multiple narrative perspectives.

Actively seek narrators to audition for the project:
Since many narrators don't stalk the audition wanted pages, reaching out may be your only chance to make them aware that the project exists.

- **Listen to auditions posted on ACX** – Even if you're going with a different company, ACX has a wide selection of narrators. While many only use ACX, most work with as many companies as possible.
- **Invite your favorites to audition** – Make sure they're in your price range and double check that you would legitimately offer this person the job. Anything else is a waste of your time and theirs.

Skip around the suggested audition samples:
No matter what criteria you use, you're likely to get thousands of matches. Many will be different samples from the same narrator. Unless you have a lot of time on your hands, I doubt you want to spend a few months wading through audition samples. Listen to a

few at random, skip a few pages, and listen to some new ones. Make a list of people whose voices you enjoy hearing.

Change the search criteria:

If you're not satisfied with the results from your first search, go back and start over. When you search, you could just leave it as male or female, but you can also narrow down by types of project accepted, pay range, and style of the sample.

It doesn't hurt to inquire about other options, but don't expect miracles:

Searching for higher PFH amounts will probably get you more experienced narrators. Let's say you can only afford to pay $50 PFH, but you're willing to try the RS$^+$ system. If you find somebody you really like but their profile says they only do jobs in the $200-$400 PFH range, send them a message describing your situation and ask if they're open to something like $50 PFH as part of an RS$^+$ deal.

You'll likely receive a polite refusal, but it doesn't hurt to ask. You never know what their current situation is. Perhaps the narrator just finished an epic 30-hour project and needs a short, very different project to avoid complete burnout. You also can't predict how your own circumstances will change. Make the connection and keep the lines of communication open. Creating an audiobook can easily take months, so don't rush into it.

It's worth reiterating that Royalty Share Plus is a fairly new concept. ACX narrators don't always keep their profiles up to date to the second. A narrator who doesn't accept straight RS projects may be open to the idea of an RS$^+$ contract.

Bonuses of actively seeking narrators:

You get a sneak peek at how well this person communicates. Sometimes, I get nothing back for a few days, but then, I receive a message that the candidate returned from vacation. You never know who you'll connect with. Even if the job doesn't work out for a particular narrator, maybe you can brighten their day by letting them know how much you enjoyed listening to their samples.

Other factors to consider:
What other projects has this narrator been involved with?
Versatile is great, but not always the best for your marketing endeavors. Many who perform adult content do so under a different name. Some don't bother. This won't be a huge concern for most, but if you're writing for middle schoolers, you probably don't want every other title credited to the narrator having a picture of a muscular, half-naked man on the front. When you look the narrator up on Audible.com, the kinds of projects that pop up can be very revealing (pun sort of intended).

What is the narrator's background and training?
The number of audiobooks a narrator has produced is interesting, though usually not the make or break point. Everybody needs to start somewhere. It's very common to find somebody with many years of acting experience, but relatively little to show on the audiobooks front. Part of the fun of searching for narrators is finding fresh voices to fall in love with. I've worked with people trained in theater and in other forms of acting. Both backgrounds have led to strong performances.

Do you like the sound and cadence of the candidate's voice?
The quality of the voice is only part of the equation. How the person reads can influence how much you enjoy the performance. If cadence didn't matter, audiobooks would be churned out by the hundreds of thousands every day simply by letting a computer program dictate into a digital recorder. Thus far, cadence is the dividing line between living person and soulless machine. Always remember, that if you do the job correctly, you will be listening to this person a lot in the coming weeks and months.

Understand the power of your invitation:

At the risk of sounding blatantly obvious, do not send an invitation to audition unless you are 100% willing and able to offer this person a contract. It will be tempting to fire off invitations to everybody with a pretty voice but understand that you're asking this person to invest part of their life on the chance at getting the job. Don't do that on a whim.

Conclusion:

At some point, the narrator you hire will have to read every portion of your book. The audition script should be representative of the whole book. You'll want to test the narrator's abilities to handle both normal descriptive passages as well as dialogue for your main character and some of the side characters. In short, you need to know if the narrator can handle the book.

Chapter 9:
Step #3: Selecting a Narrator

Introduction:

Hearing auditions for your story can quickly flip from a euphoric experience to tediousness defined, but it's also one of the most crucial steps of the audiobook making machine. The narrator will understandably make or break the baby audiobook-to-be. Best advice I can give is take your time, thoroughly vet each candidate, consider your options, and make an informed decision.

Biggest mistake you can make:

Rushing. Especially the first time, you will be very tempted to fire a contract at the first decent candidate. I still struggle with this point. These days, the process takes about a week from start to finish. This usually provides enough time for each interested candidate to put together an audition.

(Some of) the many what ifs …
What if nobody auditions?

That's the fear talking. Seriously, a lack of auditions means you're not waiting long enough or there's something wrong with your pitch. Many factors could be scaring off the candidates.

Possible pitch problems:
- **The (lack of) money** – If you're offering straight RS, expect a lower amount of auditions. Do not lie about what you intend to pay. However, if you can't afford a high PFH rate, you're going to have to talk up other points.
  Soap box moment – Royalty Share is a partnership. You've written a book you firmly believe in, and you're inviting somebody into your world to breathe a different kind of life into the story. What makes your story worth a few weeks to several months of this person's time in addition to the out-of-pocket costs they may incur?
- **The audition script** – It's worth double checking that the audition script is the best one you can muster. Don't be afraid to choose another excerpt if one isn't attracting any auditions.
- **The manuscript** – Savvy narrators will do some research on your book before auditioning for a project. The story scope is not always apparent from an excerpt. Not much you can change about that, but perhaps you are being overly ambitious with your project choice. Consider leaving the auditions open for this one and starting the process for an easier manuscript.
- **Unrealistic terms** – I am a proponent of clearly presenting your desires, but if you say something like "I need this 87,000-word manuscript made into an audiobook by next month," you are going to scare people away.

If you have a combination of these factors, expect to wait a while.

What if somebody randomly auditions?

Go with it. This is a good thing. If you have a competitive pitch, you're almost guaranteed to get random auditions. I'm defining random auditions as those not generated by your personal invitations to audition for the role.

Does that really work?

Yes. It never occurred to me to send invitations the first time I commissioned an audiobook, so the only auditions I received were completely random. I know of at least two other instances where the person hired for the job came from a random audition. In fact, I was about to send somebody a contract when I received the notification of Reuben Corbett's audition for *Spirit's Bane*. He's about to do the sequel for that book.

What if you don't like the auditions received?

Extend your timeline for hiring a narrator. Send out more invitations to audition. There's nothing wrong with multiple rounds of invitations. Adjust your pitch. If you like somebody's audition but aren't crazy about something they did in the audition, have a conversation with them. See if the thing that annoyed you can be addressed. I wouldn't go as far as asking for a second audition, but if it's a dialogue issue or something that could be demonstrated easily, see what they think of the idea. The person may be willing to make the adjustments you want. You won't know unless you inquire.

What if you receive an absolutely awful audition?

There's no written law that you must listen to every second of the submitted auditions. The reasons you may not hire somebody are many and varied. The purpose of the audition is to determine whether or not you want to partner with this narrator. If the answer is no, move on. Don't post about it. Don't complain about it. Silently make the decision and check out other candidates. The person you're rejecting will be submitting to many other projects over the course of their careers. They will win some bids and lose others.

What if you can't afford your top pick's rates?

Explain the situation to the narrator. Maybe they'll work with you on a payment plan. If you've done your part right, there should not be any surprises for the narrator, so if they submitted an audition anyway, it likely means he or she is willing to chat with you.

What if you have an overwhelming amount of auditions?

That's a good problem. I think the highest number of auditions I received for a project was thirty. At 5-6 minutes each, that's a lot of listening time. Luckily, they didn't come in all at once, so I got to hear them over the course of a few days. I also didn't listen to each of them completely. If something about the audio quality or voice indicated a poor fit for the story, I stopped listening. The point is to narrow the list down, so once you decide on the audition, your obligation to listen to it ends.

What if the narrator you really want isn't available for three months?

Ask yourself if the narrator's worth waiting for. Making audiobooks is a long game. Even if you come to an agreement this second, offer a contract, and have a speedy narrator who can churn out that book in a week or two, you're easily looking at a month before the project completes.

The good ones are worth waiting for, but if you're absolutely bound to get the party started as close to instantly as humanly possible, see if one of the other candidates has a schedule that can accommodate you.

What if the narrator you wish to work with is terrible at communicating?

Communication is vital to any relationship. It's especially true for something like creating audiobooks because you may not even live in the same time zone as the person you're hiring to work on your book.

Things to consider when it comes to communicating via messenger or email:
- ACX's messenger is clunky.
- Messages and emails can bounce or get lost in a flood of other missives.

- Not everybody lives and breathes with a phone in hand, checking email every third second. Some do. I might be close. Give people adequate time to respond. Twenty-four hours is a good starting point.
- Life often gets in the way of email time. When unexpected crises happen, checking email gets bumped way down the priorities list.
- Communication's a two-way thing. If you expect to be out of touch, let the narrator know.
- Things only improve when both parties understand there's an issue. If you have concerns about how well your narrator candidates are responding to messages, raise them. Some may diagnose you as incurably meddlesome and needy and run away, but that too can be for the best.

What if you have several amazing auditions and can't make up your mind?

Narrow your list of top candidates down to two or three and message each of these people. Let them know that they are your frontrunners for the job, so you'd like to discuss details with them.

What will communicating with the top candidates accomplish?
- You will get a feel for how well they communicate.
- You get the chance to know the narrators a little better.
- You may be able to discover whose timeframe lines up best with your vision.

Is there a downside to communicating with top candidates?
Absolutely. Most books require only one narrator. If you're talking to a few top people, that means you're going to disappoint somebody. That can be very difficult, but it's a part of the business that every narrator with any experience has come to grips with already.

Have you ever hired the runner-up?
Yes. One time, the chosen narrator had to back out for personal reasons. At her request, I ended that contract and offered it to the other narrator. Having already been in communication with her helped with that transition.

How do you narrow down the auditions?

On ACX's platform you get the chance to "like" auditions. Doing so will pull it over under a separate tab for "liked" auditions. If you end up with over a dozen auditions, this separation can prove very handy.

Reasons to not "like" an audition:

- **Narrator doesn't fit the character** – The person who auditions could sound too old, too young, too peppy, too gloomy, or something else entirely. Nearly every voice is unique. That's partly what makes the hunt for the perfect voice exciting. A voice that doesn't fit your book will be perfectly suited for somebody else's book. There's nothing wrong with rejecting an audition because it's wrong for the project.

- **Narrator reads with a weird cadence** – This one might seem harsher, but you will be listening to this person a lot. You must love everything about how they read.
- **Narrator makes a lot of reading mistakes** – I'd place less importance on this one if everything else fits, but it's still a point to consider. You should be proofreading the work anyway, but it's easier to do when there are less mistakes.
- **The audition sounds like it's being read into a tin can** – Poor audio quality would be the first reason that leaps to mind when it comes to why something gets rejected. I'm not saying you should automatically tell the person their audio quality is trash, but they may not be aware.
- **There are an excessive number of weird noises throughout the audition** – This is another quality control issue. It's less important than the whole thing sounding tinny and can probably be cleared up by some solid editing, but it could be an indicator that the narrator's skills in that area aren't quite what they should be.

  Note: It's tempting to think that ACX's quality controls will deal with stray noises. I think their check is more about making sure the sound stays above and below certain thresholds. The responsibility for turning in a clean file belongs to the audiobook creators.

Peachy. But how do you choose the one?

You could go with a pros and cons list for each candidate. Personally, I ask a few trusted friends—who happen to know the business—to give me their opinions. That may be an advantage I have that you don't. You'll have to find a way to make that decision for yourself. Odds are excellent that if the narrator made it to your top two or three, he or she will be able to complete the job to your satisfaction.

Factors I consider when choosing a narrator:
- **Budget** – Since I've determined the project budget before launching a narrator search, presumably I only receive auditions from people willing to work within that budget.
- **Character details** – The main character's occupation, attitude, and action may factor into the calculation.
- **Personal preference** – Whether I like a voice or not is completely subjective. Usually, the problem is that I like too many of the auditions.
- **Subject matter (especially in nonfiction)** – Thus far, I have only commissioned two nonfiction projects to become audiobooks. (Unless you're listening to this. In that case, welcome to audiobook inception.) The first was *5 Steps to Better Blurbs* and the second was *5 Steps to Surviving Chemistry*. For both books, I opened auditions to male and female candidates. The blurb book happened to go to a woman, while the chemistry book happened to go to a man. Most likely, the winner will be the best fit for the batch. If you open auditions a month later, you'll get a whole new crop and another top pick.
- **Narrator ability vs. number of characters** – Certain books have more characters than others. I would consider fiction projects more demanding than nonfiction ones. I like seeking narrators who have a wide range of unique character voices.
- **Narrator availability and the project timeline** – Because I try to keep myself busy, I'm not in a rush to finish, so I let my top pick decide on the dates since everything's contingent on their availability. Some people do this as their day job, so they're always looking to line up new projects.
  Side note: Being flexible is great, but also respect the narrator's time. If they're relying on you to approve the files, get to them in a timely fashion. If you can't review the files for some reason, contact them to explain the delay. These people often wait until after the project to be paid. It's not nice to hold them up indefinitely.

Tie breakers I do NOT recommend:
- **Fans** – I think I saw an ACX promo video once that recommended doing this. I disagree. It may seem like a cool thing to have your fans decide who voices the book, but it strikes me as a bad idea for multiple reasons. One, you can't please everybody. Feelings could get hurt. Two, you shouldn't air auditions with the public. Privately sharing with a professional who knows the business is very different than posting in a place where you immediately lose control over the file's location. Three, you don't want to damage anybody's reputation. That could lead to legal trouble later.
- **Family** – If family wants to be involved because they're happy for you, awesome, but don't tie the book's fate to them. If for some reason things don't work out, that could get awkward.
- **Coin flips** – Don't leave somebody's fate to that much chance.

You've chosen a narrator … now what?
- **Contact your top choice** – I recommend messaging the narrator and asking which terms they want in the contract. These things include when the First 15 minutes will post and when the project should be completed. They should pad that with a few weeks, but the contract dates are guidelines, not set in stone. Also, the contact lets them know you're going to send a contract soon, so they can watch for it.
- **Send the contract** – This should take a few minutes as every question and term should already be settled. The questions you'll be asked to fill out in the form have to do with the payment system, the relevant dates, and whether you'll be distributing exclusively through ACX or plan to post it elsewhere too.
- **Wait for the narrator to accept the contract.** – ACX recommends a 48-hour window. It's usually only taken about 12-24 hours for the contracts to be accepted.

- **Tactfully inform the other people who auditioned that you've found a narrator.** – If you go to any audition on the project page, there should be a place there for you to send the candidate a message. This step might not directly affect the way your project runs, but it should win you more "positive human" points. It's also the polite thing to do. You have no idea who you'll want to invite to audition for other projects. Those conversations go better when they don't remember you as "that inconsiderate jerk."

Conclusion:

Choose your narrator wisely. He or she will be your partner throughout the project. I suspect nothing in this section was shocking to you. Most of the turnoffs I mentioned would likely spring up naturally. Take your time with this phase of the journey.

Chapter 10:
Step #4: Maintaining Clear Lines of Communication

Introduction:

Every relationship, even business ones, can be improved by facilitating great communication. Truth is, you could do everything right and things can—and will—still go wrong. The first step in fixing an issue is realizing its existence. In addition, a lack of communication can let small issues fester into larger ones.

The balance you should strike:

You want to be supportive of the narrator without being stalkery. Check in. Get to know them. Let them know of changes in your life that may affect them. For example, I'm a high school teacher. That means, that for two glorious summer months, I have a lot of time to devote to checking audiofiles. Come September, my free time diminishes rapidly. In turn, that can affect my turnaround time in reviewing files.

Communicate in the way that's most comfortable to you and the narrator:

This might be the first topic you should discuss. The initial contact probably happened through a messaging system or email. Email will likely be the preferred form of communication from there on out. However, phones are also an option. Having recently worked collaboratively with somebody on a book project, I can confidently say that there's a time and place for phone conversations.

I much prefer email, but if the narrator's more comfortable discussing some details via the phone, go with the flow.

Things to talk about before, during, and after files are recorded:
Preparation topics:
- **Manuscript** – Having been burned by other projects, some narrators insist on reading the entire project before agreeing to sign a contract. That's relatively rare. Many agree based on your description and a few informal conversations about the rest of the book. However, before recording, the narrator will need to read the whole book. You'll have to send them the project in the electronic form of their choosing.
- **Character notes** – The narrator will likely have their own special system for marking up a manuscript with notes on how to approach various sections, but you should help them at the beginning by providing character notes.
- **Content warnings** – The preliminary talks with the narrator should reiterate anything possibly controversial. If a narrator says that they won't read profanities, consider mentioning anything that would be considered borderline. People's definitions of profanity can differ, so it's best to be thorough. Ideally, these conversations should have happened before a contract was signed.
- **Recording schedule** – You should have a rough idea of when they'll be sending you files so you can get to them in a timely fashion. It's rude to give them a deadline and then be lax in when and how you give them feedback.

What could* go into character notes?
*Please note that I said *could* in this section. You may wish to ask the narrator if they even want your character notes. Most will say yes because they want to know your thoughts. They've been hired to help realize your vision for the story, so it helps to know where you're coming from.

- **Accents** – If a character should have a specific accent, it needs to be mentioned in the notes. Try not to go overboard with this. If your book has a ton of vital accents, be honest about the demands of the job before seeking a narrator, especially if your budget consists of appreciation and peanuts.
- **Dialogue** – Only include small snippets that demonstrate a point you're trying to make.
- **Comparisons** – This one can be the most helpful but understand that you won't get an exact replica. I once described a character as being like Agent Scully from the X-Files. The comparison is meant to give the narrator a starting point in developing the voice they'll use for the character.
- **Physical description** – This can help the narrator form a fuller picture of who they're voicing. The choices they make in voicing a scrawny ten-year-old boy will be vastly different than a battle-hardened Army Ranger.
- **Relevant background** – They may not need to know the character's favorite meal, but if that's a crucial point of the mystery novel, mention it. Like real people, characters have defining moments, events that shape their actions and motivations.
- **Emotional disposition** – In order to convey the character properly, the narrator will have to understand the character's attitudes. Timid people talk differently than ticked off people. These things should be apparent in the book itself, but you want to give the narrator as much information as you can without being overwhelming.

Things to avoid with character notes.
- **Don't make them too long.** They're CliffsNotes, not PhD dissertations.
- **Don't make ridiculous demands.** Presumably, you've hired a professional. Let them do their job, but don't expect them to sound exactly like the voice you have in your head for the character.
- **Don't include every single named character.** I'm a huge proponent of the main characters and major side characters being distinguishable. But don't be afraid to let some characters be assigned a generic male or female voice.

During the recording process:
- **Progress updates** – You don't need a minute-by-minute update, but you should be informed when new files are available for review. ACX will send you an automatic message when the First 15 Minutes checkpoint gets uploaded, but they do not notify you after that until the entire book has been submitted for final review. Typically, these are quick back and forth emails about chapters being uploaded.

  Aside about the First 15 Minutes Checkpoint: I highly recommend having the narrator upload chapter 1 for this. That will save him or her time later. It doesn't have to come to 15 minutes in total. It exists as a last-ditch effort for you and the narrator to figure out if your partnership is going to work. For projects where I've worked with the narrator before and know their process, I've even had them upload chapters from other books so they could upload the current book at their leisure. I do not recommend that if you've never worked with the narrator before.
- **Pronunciation questions** – Names can be tricky to pronounce, especially if it's a fantasy world where you made up every place and character name. Your character notes should have cleared up many of these questions already, but things can come up. The English language is filled with lovely pitfalls like multiple acceptable ways of

pronouncing some words. Sometimes, these pronunciations differ based on region, so the character's circumstances could matter a great deal.

- **Life happenings and delays** – Common life events and milestones like having a baby, getting into an accident, losing a friend, celebrating a birthday, and going on vacation can throw your daily routine out of whack. You don't have to let the narrator know every time you sit down to eat, but if you're planning a backpacking trip to the Himalayas and will be out of touch for nine weeks, you might want to notify them as that will seriously mess with your availability to answer questions and check files. It follows that you don't need to know every detail of the narrator's life, but if he or she picks up a head cold and currently sounds like a disgruntled frog, your files will be delayed. Recordings are very good at picking up the difference between a voice that's almost healthy and completely healthy. There's absolutely nothing you can do about that but be understanding.

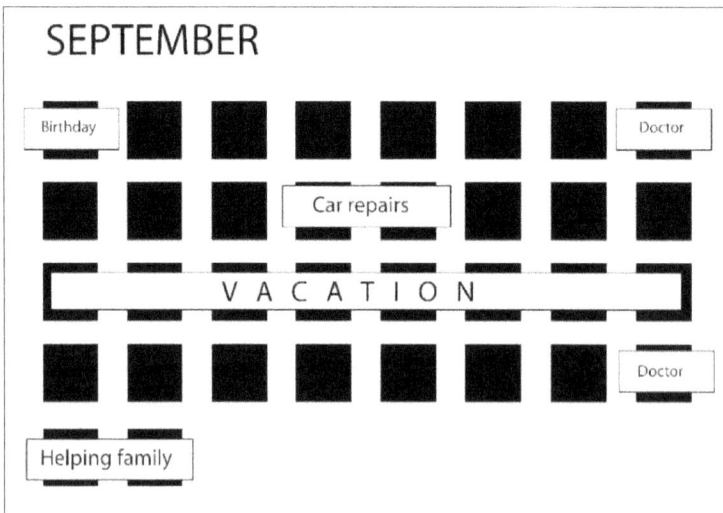

During the review phase:

I highly suggest you make this phase concurrent with the recording one. In other words, ask the narrator to upload the chapters as they are edited. The reason is twofold. It helps with catching pronunciation discrepancies early and saves time by allowing you to review while work is still being done on later chapters.

Give the narrator a timestamp as well as a brief description of the problem you're pointing out. Copy paste a small section of the manuscript. The timestamps can be difficult to pin down and off from what the narrator's hearing, so the description will let them locate what you're talking about.

Things to point out as you review your audiobook files (annotated):
- **Parts you really love** – I try to point out places where I love the inflection. The rest of the audio notes are likely going to be mistakes and things I want changed, so I try to note parts I enjoy too. A little positive feedback can go a long way. Besides, nobody wants to hear negativity all the time.
- **Character deviations** – If your narrator's doing multiple voices for characters, pay attention to the consistency.
- **Pronunciation changes** – Some vexing words have two or more legitimate ways of saying them. Which version is "correct" often gets defined regionally in a country. Many names in the fantasy genre get made up. Hopefully, the narrator asks you if they're not certain how you want a name pronounced, before saying it ninety times in the book. This is one mistake you must catch as soon as possible for everybody's sanity.
- **Unintended inflections** – Sometimes the grammar in the manuscript has a little room for interpretation and the narrator happens to go with inflection you hadn't intended. If something fails to line up with your vision, point it out. Try not to be too nitpicky. Narrators aren't mind readers. They can only work with what you've given them. If you

suddenly have three hundred things for them to change, the problem is probably with the manuscript and your expectations, not the performance.

- **Tweaks to minor characters** – You should not be asking for a switch to a main character's voice, unless it's one instance of that voice. If a minor character has two lines that are simply driving you crazy, make a note for the narrator.
- **Odd noises in the background** – Everything from errant breaths to their neighbor's dog can sometimes make it through into the file the narrator uploads. Most things will be dealt with in editing, but just as grammar mistakes slip by you, so oddball noises can sneak through the cleanup process.
- **Deviations from the manuscript** – Most narrators are gracious enough to fix places where they missed a word or added a word but consider how important the missing word or phrase is. Sometimes, it's easier to change the manuscript and republish or simply accept the addition or deletion. In many cases, the added or subtracted word doesn't change the sentence's meaning. I tend to point these out in orange or green with a comment on whether it should be changed or left alone.
  Note: If the book is about 95% accurate to the manuscript, it will likely be included in the Whispersync program. It's a cool program for readers because you can get huge discounts on audiobooks if you own the ebook version. While such steep discounts can encourage more readers to buy your book, keep in mind that you'll also take a hit in the audiobook royalties.
- **Subtle changes in the manuscript** – If there's a mistake in your book, fix it. If it's a huge, sweeping mistake try to catch it early and let the narrator know as soon as possible. I've changed manuscripts from time to time. For example, I believe the chemistry book had a mistake in one of the answers that needed to be fixed. Usually, it's a quick fix. When it happens, you should give timestamps and a

thorough explanation as to what's changing and why.

Some what ifs ...

What if the narrator wants to break the contract?

Evaluate the reason. You could try to talk the narrator out of it, but typically, your best move is to let them break the contract. Thus, I recommend not burning bridges with the other auditioners. You may need to turn to your runner-up.

This happened to me. The narrator I contracted had some life stuff spring up and needed to bow out, so I asked the other stellar auditioner to step in. It worked out great. The exact process may vary by company, but if your contract is through ACX, the pair of you will need to exchange messages through the clunky messenger system so it's official. Then, contact customer service (support@acx.com) and let them know the situation and that you've exchanged messages through the system already. They'll dissolve the old contract, leaving you open to sending a new one.

What if you want to fire a narrator?

Never had this issue, but I gather it's much the same. However, depending on how far along in the project you are, you might have to pay the narrator a kill fee for the work they've already put in. Try to work things out, but if you must break the contract and aren't sure what steps to take, contact customer service for advice.

It's very easy to break a contract if both parties agree. I'm sure it gets murkier if one party wants to keep to the contract.

What if the narrator's being stubborn about making a fix?

Take a hard look at if you're being unreasonable. Also balance the fix against the worth. I once had to ask a narrator to change the pronunciation of a character's name because the way she had it was throwing me off every time I heard it. She made the corrections without any arguing, but the splices weren't perfect.

To this day, the project still bears the awkwardness. I can easily see a narrator balking at making over fifty of the same type of adjustment. This is why the narrator should ask if they're not sure on pronouncing a name, and why you should be checking files as they get uploaded.

If the change doesn't matter, you may want to let it stand. If the editing isn't perfect, the fix could end up being worse than the subtle change. If the change matters, fight for it. You're a writer. Use your words to persuade the narrator of the necessity of the change.

What if something comes up in the narrator's life and the project needs to be delayed?

I hope the pair of you have the type of relationship where this isn't a huge issue. If the narrator needs to delay a project for a legitimate reason, try to be gracious about it. I don't know how other companies work, but with ACX, the deadlines are guidelines. They help you schedule and pace the project. However, they mean nothing as long as you and the narrator agree to any adjustments.

What are legitimate reasons?

Almost anything. The narrator catching a cold is a straightforward one, but the reason doesn't have to involve the narrator's health. They might become caretaker of a parent, have a sick child, lose a pet, or have some other stressor that flips them emotionally onto their backside.

What if I don't like the performance?

Cry. Big, fat, ugly tears.

Seriously, it shouldn't reach that point. If you've done your job correctly thus far, you should know very well what you're getting into. There's a 15-minute check on ACX and Findaway Voices. It exists as a stopgap where you and the narrator can test the waters of your partnership. Point being, I hope you're not referring to the completed project. If something about the performance bothers you, talk to the narrator.

If you are talking about the sum of the project, I suggest a phone conversation with the narrator since clearly email communication is inadequate for bridging the communications gap between you.

I also suggest taking a few days off from the project then listening to it again with fresh ears. Sometimes, that makes all the difference. It's happened to me a few times that I wasn't quite certain I liked a side character's voice. After a few listens, the chosen voice usually grows on me. In fact, it often happens that these voices become my favorites.

What if something comes up in my life and I can't handle reviewing the audiobook files?

Email the narrator and explain the situation. If the circumstance causing the holdup has no foreseeable end, investigate other alternatives. See if there's someone in your circles or the narrator's who can take over proof-listening duties. Some people do that as a side gig, so you may be able to outsource it for a reasonable fee. I'm sure the thought of an additional cost is doing wonders for your blood pressure, but it might be worth the peace of mind if you need to see it through. Maybe try to use that as your escape time. Just do a few minutes a day until it's done.

What if the narrator stops answering me?

Wait. Try to contact the narrator again and wait some more. Yes, this too happened to me. Fortunately, we hadn't begun the actual project yet, but that's where I learned you can break the contract without the narrator in extreme circumstances.

The mystery:
Caitlin Jacques narrated *Redeemer Chronicles Book 1: Awakening*. Her communication throughout that process was top-notch. I mean very detailed, thoughtful email replies were the norm. Her audio editing was some of the best I'd ever experienced. We contracted the second book, chatted about it for a bit, and then,

I got complete radio silence. I keep thinking something bad might have happened to her. Hope that's not the case, but I've resigned myself to the fact that I may never know.

So, what happened?
I dissolved the contract and found a new narrator to take over the Redeemer Chronicles series. I love the new narrator, but it would have been nicer to have the original one for consistency. I always thought you needed to have the same narrator if you're going to create an omnibus of audiobooks, but I think you can do so if you own the audiobook rights outright. This would rule out RS situations.

Both times I've had to switch narrators have occurred before the project began, so it came down to a few messages and a bit of waiting. If you're mid-project, there's the risk of losing your investment. That's the slight risk of progress payments, but I still recommend them. Keep in mind, if something ever happened to you and you don't do progress payments, the narrator might never get paid for the work.

Conclusion:
There's no way to predict the problems that could materialize. Clear lines of communication can help you deal with problems that arise. Usually, most things can be fixed with enough time, clear explanation, and understanding.

Chapter 11:
Step #5: Final Review

Introduction:

After the narrator has returned the audiofiles with every correction you asked for, it's time for the final review. This is where you hear the performance start to finish. It's partly for entertainment value, but also for doing a final check on voice continuity. You also want to make sure each chapter is safely tucked in its correct location if you're using ACX. If you use Findaway Voices, I believe the files will be locked into position already.

How does a final review differ from a normal review?

I suppose it doesn't have to differ, but for me, there can be a difference in the level of listening. I try to vary the intensity level of listening because it can point out which errors jump out and which sail under the radar.

What levels of listening are there?

- **With the manuscript** – This is the first, most intense level of listening used mostly for finding mistakes between the audiobook files and the manuscript. By the time you get to a final listen, you should be beyond this point, though it may help your attention span to read along with the audiofile.

- **Without the manuscript but not doing much else** – I rarely do this because I feel like I need to be doing something.
- **Without the manuscript and doing something else** – The something else could be a game like Candy Crush or a digital puzzle or a chore like ironing or folding laundry. I would not recommend something that involves much noise like doing the dishes because it can be hard to relisten to certain passages from a phone. The point here is to find something mindless to occupy a few brain cells while you listen.

LEVELS OF LISTENING

What am I looking for in the final review?

My final reviews tend toward the lighter listening. I want to confirm that all chapters are in their appropriate location, they are properly labeled, and they offer good entertainment value. If a noise jumps at me while I'm semi-distracted, it's worth noting to the narrator.

How important is the final review?

I suppose you could skip this, but it's a chance to hear the book as a whole. I'm not sure why you'd want to give that up. I caution against skipping this part because fixing problems once the project is approved gets much more difficult. I told you about that snafu with a file saying it was chapter one but being the prologue repeated. We got it sorted—I think—but it took months of back and forth messages with and without ACX's customer support to get the correct files loaded. If I had been more careful with my review back then, we could have avoided that exercise in frustration.

Do I need to use a manuscript for it?
It really depends on your purpose. If you want to make sure everything's perfect, it may help to have the manuscript. If your main purpose is to gauge the entertainment value, then not having the manuscript can help. You can download the files and take them on a walk with you. I prefer to do all the listening from my browser.

What if I find a mistake?
Tell the narrator and ask for a fix. You'll have to make a judgment call on the importance of the fix. Try asking for a second opinion. I got to a point in listening to one file that I could swear there was a noise in one spot. There might have been, but I asked somebody who'd never heard the files to listen and see if anything bothered her. She listened to the whole section without any complaint. Use this method with caution though because the uninitiated probably don't know what they're listening for. A lot could slip by them. In that situation, I decided to let the minor noise remain because I was aware how hyperaware I'd become by that point.

If something needed to be fixed, do I have to do another final review?
I suppose the answer comes down to how many perfectionist tendencies you have. You may wish to listen to that file start to finish, but if nothing has been altered in the other files, they should be fine to leave.

Conclusion:
I see the final review as the culmination of the project. The rest of the review process might be seen as work, but this should be taken

as the reward. It's the moment where at last that dream of hearing your book as an audiobook gets fulfilled.

Chapter 12:
Bonus 1: Things Rights Holders Should and Shouldn't Do

Introduction:

Much of the information in the chapter can be found scattered throughout the book, but I think there's value in putting everything in one place. I've taken the liberty of asking some narrators for their opinions on do's and don'ts. If the information came from a blog, it will be linked at the end of the book.

Some Don'ts:

(Courtesy of Jeffrey Kaffer's Blog post unless noted)

- **Be a lousy communicator** – If the narrator has questions about your project, answer them in a timely fashion!

- **Ask for multiple narrators on a Royalty Share project** – There's a time and place for RS. But the concept is a big enough risk for one person to shoulder, let alone cutting that hypothetical pie in half again.
- **Always expect music or sound effects** – This one's tricky. I have some projects with music and some without. I've heard some books with sound effects, yet most are without. From what I can tell, music and sound effects have the potential to enhance the project, but—and that's a big but—you're more likely to tick off a listener by having music and sound effects. Trust me, been on that side too. When they work, they're lovely, and when sound effects go awry, it ruins the whole experience.
- **Ask for an audition over ten minutes in length** – The rough math places this in the 1,500-word range. I still vote for around 1,000 words. That's about 5-6 minutes. It's long enough to get a feel for the narrator's talent, yet short enough not to break you in the process of choosing a top audition.
- **Offer a project as RS or PFH** (Gina Rogers) – I will admit to having done this. The difference is that I genuinely offered both options. And when I run a RS project, I pay a bonus that makes it a hybrid project anyway. Most people chose the PFH if given the choice. The uncool part of this is that most who offer RS or PFH do so with the notion that they're really only going to offer RS, but posting as PFH will garner more interest. As previously discussed, it's not a nice thing to do.
- **Leave the comments section blank in the audition setup** (Persephone Rose) – Giving the narrator a little to work with can make the auditioning process easier.
- **Expect the narrator to sound like the voice in your head** (Petrea Burchard, Paul Heitsch, and many others) – There will be variation. In matters of pronunciation, you can ask for specifics, but voice quality isn't going to change that much. Most narrators are going to default to their natural reading voice for most of the narrative.

- **Offer a lousy PFH** (me) – Lousy's open to some interpretation. From what I can tell, the bare minimum of PFH that won't get you thrown out on your ear is $150. If you have a short project, consider a higher PFH.
- **Offer a RS$^+$ if you have no clue what that is** (Gina Rogers) – Royalty Share Plus is the latest bid for legitimization of hybrid projects. It's a type of contract that will allow the royalties to be split with the narrator. The difference between this and a traditional RS project is who bears the financial risks. In normal RS, the narrator shoulders all financial risks. In a RS$^+$ agreement, the rights holder pays to offset the production costs. I'm assuming it's a smaller PFH amount rather than a flat fee, but I've personally never done it before. Major point is that if you offer RS$^+$, expect to have a frank discussion about how much you're willing to pay for the project.
- **Hide the demands of the project** (Austenne Grey) – It can be a problem if you present an audition script with only two to three characters but have a book that demands twenty-five distinct voices with most being different accents. It's never a great start to a relationship to hide a pertinent detail. You might be tempted to think you'll never find a narrator if you're upfront, but if somebody's scared off by that kind of challenge, they would likely be a bad fit for your project.

Some Do's:

- **Always do the math ahead of time** – (9,300-ish words = 1 audiobook hour) You should know what you're getting into.
- **State what your PFH will be** (Gina Rogers) – ACX has a range, but there's a gigantic difference between a $200 PFH project and one that will pay $400.
- **Always include an audition script** (Bob McCoy) – It never occurred to me that somebody would skip that, but I'm told that sometimes people ask for general samples. You can find samples on ACX or the narrator's website. First, this makes you look lazy. Second, if you're going to choose the best voice for the book, you really need to hear what they can do with that exact manuscript, not some other random piece of writing.
- **Make sure the audition script is properly formatted** (Write Scribe) – ACX is great, but some of their copy-paste boxes can leave you with a globby mess. The narrators will appreciate having a ready to go audition script.
- **Have a clean manuscript** (Suzanne Barbetta) – Having to fix grammar issues on the fly slows down the work.

- **Check with experts when it comes to foreign languages** (Suzanne Barbetta) – Google Translate doesn't count. I will confess to relying on that, though to be honest, I try to avoid foreign languages where possible. Unless it's fantasy, then the foreign language exists in my head. If that's the case, it's probably phonetic because that's how my brain works.
- **Always seek to improve communication with the narrator** (Kerry McCurdy, Laura Bannister, many others) – Be direct yet respectful. You're working with a professional, so treat them as such.
- **Be willing to pay for quality work** – Even if you can't afford a decent PFH, try to pay the narrator something.
- **Be willing to review the files** – You have a vested interest in turning out the best possible project. Take ownership of the project. You've hired somebody because you either lacked the skills or the will to bring the book to life with your own voice. Invest your time and talents into making it the best possible listening experience it can be.
- **Freely dole out praise** (Aven Shore) – A lot of what you'll be telling the narrator involves nitpicking mistakes and correcting pronunciation. If you find something you like, point it out. Praise doesn't necessarily pay bills, but it encourages the narrator, which is always good. As a professional, the narrator will do the job even when they don't really feel like it, but anything you as a rights holder can do to make that job easier will always be appreciated.

Conclusion:

There's a lot involved in the process of bringing an audiobook into existence. Do everything in your power to make the journey as painless as possible for yourself and the narrator.

Chapter 13:
Bonus 2: Introduction to Audiobook Promotions and Networking

Disclaimer: I do not claim to have cracked the code to selling massive amounts of audiobooks. In truth, some of that may be linked to genre, cover, description, and everything else that goes into selling a story as an ebook or a paperback.

Introduction:

Promoting an audiobook can be difficult. There aren't as many ways to advertise, and at times, it's a harder concept to sell to people. Network with authors and narrators to discover and take advantage of the opportunities that exist.

Why is promoting audiobooks so difficult?

It's more difficult than promoting ebooks and paperbacks. Ebooks have the advantage of many very popular newsletter promotion opportunities. Paperbacks can be sold directly to a person at a convention, street fair, or other vendor opportunity. Audiobooks as discussed here are a digital product that's less popular than ebooks.

Why are audiobooks less popular than ebooks?

- Odds are good that fans of audiobooks are also fans of ebooks and paperbacks, but the reverse isn't always true.

- Some people don't like them because they've had bad experiences with audiobooks.
- Some people read much faster than an audiobook's playback speed. You can fix some of that by messing with the playback speed, but then the narrator will sound like a caffeinated squirrel.
- The audiobook format is easier to ignore. Thus, it's easier to lose one's place and harder to backtrack to figure out what's what.
- Audiobooks are harder to publish, and therefore, are more expensive. Libraries and other apps offering a variety of audiobooks are gaining popularity, but unless you know where to look, it can still be more expensive than ebooks.

But don't despair, audiobooks are becoming way more popular because they have advantages over ebooks and paperbacks. You can enjoy the stories without spending the time reading. In that sense, they're easier to indulge in than ebooks.

How do you promote an audiobook?
ACX gives you free codes to promote the title. Once upon a time, ACX gave out codes that could be used on any book. The new ACX codes are specific to the title. If your audiobook is brand new, it will not be given royalty-producing codes, but you can—and should—still use them to generate reviews. I believe Author's Direct also does something similar with codes. That's the site you'll be on if you make a book through Findaway Voices.

Disclaimer: Prices are a fickle thing. Be aware that as soon as I publish a price, it could be obsolete due to the ever-changing nature of the business.

How do you find people to give a free code to?

- **Post it at https://audiofreebies.com/** – Single title listings are $10 and series listings are $15. The ability to post an entire series is amazing. I tried it with three series and have fulfilled over 40 requests. With this site, you get an email informing you of somebody's interest in your series. Like any ad, it's only very effective the first week or so after posting, but occasionally, I still get requests for an older listing. Highly recommended. My criteria for an effective ad is one that can pay for itself then turn a nice profit. Pro: High interaction with the listener. Con: It's up to you to find a free code on your dashboard and fulfill the request. Depending on the number of requests, this could get time consuming, but trust me, it's a great problem to have.

- **Post it at http://audiobooksunleashed.com/** - This site was formerly https://www.freeaudiobookpromocodes. com/. (I'm told the FAPC site will forward to the other eventually, but the switch may not have even happened yet.) Regardless, I also highly recommend this one. There are several prices, but I believe the best one if you have a lot of titles is six months for $150. Seems steep, but it may help to think of it as $25 a month. The nice thing about this site is that you put every code you have into a google form. When somebody requests the code, they're automatically kicked the next code in line. Pro: Incredibly easy! Con: No interaction with the listener.

- **Social media announcements** – There are a ton of Facebook groups whose only purpose is to have authors and narrators post available titles and people request those free codes. Pro: High interaction with the listener. Also, it's free. Just abide by the rules of the various Facebook groups (or other social media platform gathering place). Con: Probably the most "labor intensive" of the ad types.

- **Audiobook Boom** – This is one of the few effective newsletter promotions focused on audiobooks. You pay a fee. I believe the fee is currently $12, but you can expect that to go up as the years go on. In return, you get the title, cover, and basic book facts listed in the weekly newsletter. People who subscribe will request titles. You'll receive a list of everybody who has requested your book. It's up to you to make the contact to get them the code and follow up to see if they reviewed. I've had mixed success with this one. I'm hearing the owner of this list will also run an ad site like the three listed above.

- **Audiobook Edge** – This is both a Facebook group and a newsletter. I know the most about it because I run it. The concept is like Audiobook Boom with a few distinct differences. First, it's free. Second, I only offer clean reads to the list, so I personally listen to everything that's offered through there. Third, the newsletter is monthly because that's about the limit of what I can personally vet. Fourth, if I like your book, you'll always get a review from me, but if the book's not clean, I refuse to list it.

- **Blog tour/website feature** – I've had very limited success with these things, but to be fair, I've only tried it once or twice. Generally, this works by you paying somebody a small fee to run the blog tour for you. The coordinator will usually put your book title and a brief writeup on their website and then arrange for a handful of other bloggers to post similar features on their blogs over the course of a few days. The main issue is that people who specialize in this are rare and flooded with titles. So, your book sits with every other person who's ever paid this blog tour coordinator. You also have to trust that the blogs to have a strong enough following of people who like the genre of book you've written.

It's not a competition:
I'd encourage you to use each of these methods as often as feasible. Audiobook Boom, website promotions, and blog tours will have varying levels of success for different titles. There's also a cost involved. Social media announcements are great, but you need to spend time interacting in the right Facebook groups to make meaningful connections. Audiobook Edge is free but a way slower process than some of the other methods.

How do I give somebody a code?
ACX has tried to streamline this process.

Step-by-step procedure for giving somebody an ACX code:
- Go to www.acx.com.
- Find the About ACX tab and click the dropdown menu. Select promotional codes.
- Click "Get My Codes."
- Find the book title and click "Get Promo Codes."
- You can sort codes by region or see all available. Find an unused code and tap the "Copy" button. Be sure to also click the sliding button that indicates you shared this code already to avoid giving the same code to multiple people.

Why connect with other authors and narrators?

Misery loves company. I'm kidding, but there is value in finding people who understand the frustrations and challenges you face. Plus, there's a wealth of information out there, and you won't find it if you don't ask the right questions to the right people. Being part of those conversations can expand your knowledge base and may even introduce you to your next narrator.

Where do you connect with other authors and narrators?

- **ACX profiles** – ACX has a ton of narrator samples. Even if you don't intend to use the site to make an audiobook, it's a great resource for exploring various narrators. Many will have their personal websites listed.
- **Personal websites** – You can also find people's websites by searching for them. If you're listening to an audiobook and want to check into the narrator, do a little research. They're usually easy to find if they have a website.
- **Facebook groups** – There's a group out there for almost everything. Certain groups are a tad more intense than others, but if you're willing to ask questions, you'll most likely find people willing to give you answers.

What are some of those Facebook groups you mentioned?

I will put in the hyperlinks, but you can always find these groups by using the search bar in Facebook.

For connecting with authors and narrators:
- Audiobook Lovers
- Audiobook Edge Authors/Narrators
- Indie (ACX and Others) Audiobook Narrators and Producers
- Clean Indie Reads

For connecting with readers:
- Audiobook Addicts
- Audiobook Edge Reader Discussion Group
- Get FREE audiobooks for honest reviews!
- Free Audiobook Codes for Honest Reviews

There's probably a lot of overlap in the groups, but it's worth checking out and joining multiple groups.

Conclusion:

There's no magic press-here-to-sell-a-million-audiobooks button, though if you find it, please email me. If you form meaningful connections with the right people, you can find a way to use a lot of those audiobook free codes. They do not count as a royalty-producing sale anymore, but it is important that you develop meaningful connections with readers and get them to leave a review for your audiobook.

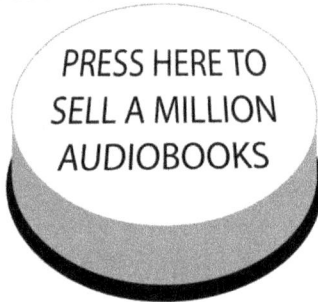

Chapter 14:
Bonus 3: Basics of Audiobook Email Writing

Introduction:

Email will likely be your primary means of communication with the narrator. Whether you like the method or not, it's easy for each party to answer in their own time and has the advantage of letting you think about your responses before issuing them. Some of them can be form letters, but you still want it to sound like an individual missive. The personal touch can go a long way in establishing a meaningful connection.

What kinds of emails and messages will you have to prepare?

- Invitation to audition
- Project description's additional comments
- Top candidate notification and details discussion
- Thank you notes for everybody who auditioned
- Discussion of timeline and payment
- General check-ins and progress updates

Anatomy of an invitation to audition email:

I will put a sample invitation letter as one of the appendices. Before then, let's look at what you should cover when you write your invitation email.

- **Opener** – You should discuss how you came across their name. In many cases this will be by listening to some of their audio samples on ACX. You can personalize the letter by telling them exactly which sample caught your attention. This can also be helpful if the person auditions for you because they will have a better handle on what you enjoy.
- **Book details** – You do not need to put the full blurb here, but you may wish to put a link there so the narrator can seek more details and read reviews. The main purpose of this section is to let them know what's up for grabs. You should include important details like word count and overall tone.
- **Enticement** – Give the narrator reasons to want to work with you. What are you offering? Royalty Share, a great pay-per-finished hour rate, a hybrid deal? Remember, that unless your book has hit several of the big-time bestseller lists, it's probably not a great candidate for Royalty Share. It's best if you can offer a competitive PFH rate, but that's not the only thing you can offer. RS^+ is a viable option these days. Being a good communicator and being easy to work with are also things that will endear you to potential candidates.
- **Audition details** – You should put something in about how long the audition window will stay open. My projects tend to be cast within a week. That's usually enough time for those who wish to enter to pull their audition together.
- **Invitation** – They'll get the point, but it never hurts to close out with a formal invitation to audition.
- **Closing salutation** – You can switch to more casual signoffs later, but your invitation should have a formal, friendly tone.

ANATOMY OF AN EMAIL

OPENER

BOOK DETAILS

ENTICEMENT

AUDITION DETAILS

INVITATION

CLOSING
SALUTATION

Project description's additional comments section:

This should say almost the same thing as the invitation, but it goes in the comments section to inform those who find the project by search. I've never seen ACX from that side because I'm not a narrator, but I am told that they have filter options to narrow down audition opportunities. They can select from genre, gender, compensation, accents, languages, word count, and even ACX sales rank, if that's still a thing. I will add a sample letter to the first appendix so you can see the difference.

What's a top candidate notification and what kinds of details should we discuss?

This type of email is what I'm calling the negotiation phase. When you've found a few awesome auditions, you should contact the top contenders and chat about the possibilities. Be clear if you're contacting multiple people. They should all be aware that it's not a done deal at this point, but that they did make it through round one of your consideration.

Questions that should be addressed:
- **What is the narrator's availability?** – Not everybody can start right away. If the narrator is doing this for a living or trying to get as many projects as possible, he or she will likely keep a few projects lined up at any given time. For some, that could mean a delay of a few weeks before they can begin, and for others, it could mean your book would be held up a few months. The importance of a quick start rests mainly with you. To me, finding the right voice matters more, so I'm willing to wait a month or more as necessary.
- **Is the narrator available for the payment terms you're offering?** – If you were clear in your invitation and description, this should be a formality. For me, it's a matter of discussing the options. I've found most opt for the higher PFH instead of the lower PFH plus bonuses because of the straightforward nature of the deal.
- **Can the narrator handle the project?** – If you didn't get a chance to describe the project in fuller detail, this would be the place to outline some of the demands. Even if it's been covered before, this is a good time to mention if there are multiple accents and how many major characters need a voice. If I remember correctly, this came up once. I raised concerns when talking with the candidates for *Beyond Broken Pencils*. It's a story about a school shooting, so naturally, there are a ton of characters, both male and female. Since the narrator I hired was male, I needed to

know if he could handle that.

- **Is the narrator responsive?** – It's not a direct question, but it gets answered by this step. Sending and receiving messages from the narrator shows you their response time and how they present themselves. A breakdown in communication at this stage doesn't necessarily deal a deathblow to the idea of working with the person, but it's something to be aware of moving forward.

Is sending thank you notes a skippable step?

Of course, but I don't recommend skipping this step. Yes, it can be tedious depending on how many auditions were received. It may require an hour of your life, but remember, everybody who auditioned for your book probably also spent an hour of their life preparing, recording, and refining a viable sample for you. Besides, you may want to work with some of these people in the future. It never hurts to be polite. Most are understanding about the nature of the business.

Why is discussion of timeline and payment a separate thing? Didn't we just cover that?

If you only sent a top candidate notification to one person, then you're correct. This is likely something you can skip. I'm assuming the previous top candidate notification went to at least two people. Before you send a live contract, you should ask the narrator to give you the dates for the First 15 checkpoint and which date the project should be due. Even though these dates are guidelines, I usually pad their estimate for the final project by a few weeks. If the narrator can deliver ahead of schedule, awesome. Psychologically, it's nicer if they're able to complete the project early. It's the same logic of shipping estimates. If you need to ship something across the country, always pad the delivery by a day or two. When it shows up on time, you look good. If it takes a day longer, it's still "on time."

Check-ins and progress updates:

These messages should be short and casual. When you finish reviewing some chapters, you should send the notes to the narrator. If you're going to need longer to review files, tell the narrator. He or she may not need every detail, but it's nice to keep them in the loop on anything that could affect them. Many do this as a side gig because they enjoy it, but just as many or more do this for a living. Never mess with a person's livelihood if you can help it. You owe the narrator at least a head's up about delays, especially if you're not paying until the end of the project. (This is how a SAG-AFTRA contract works. When the book's complete, you mail a check off to the company, and they will pay the narrator on your behalf.)

General rule of thumb with creating an audiobook:

Never be in a hurry when it comes to deadlines. You're at the mercy of a lot of factors. Keep in constant communication and be understanding when life messes with the precious schedule.

Conclusion:

Even if you didn't have this cheat sheet of types of missives you should send to the narrator, you'd probably do most of them instinctively. Understand that tone can be harder to pinpoint in an email, so you have to be more careful with your wording. In hiring a narrator, you've invited a partner into your life to share the passion you have for your story. The relationship may require some work, but it's well-worth the investment of time and effort. Be clear, understanding, and supportive to the best of your abilities. Like writing, audiobooks are addictive. You probably won't be able to resist making more, so do everything in your power to be the best rights holder you can possibly be.

Chapter 15:
Bonus 4: Seeing Both Sides

Introduction:

You'll find that authors and narrators hold some very strong opinions on quite a few issues concerning the audiobook world. I'm really trying to avoid an us vs. them mentality. This section will attempt to point out and comment on a few of the hot-button topics. I won't say too much on the money issue, but for perspective, I thought it'd be good to show you one narrator's breakdown of a PFH job.

Where'd the money go? One narrator's experience.

The narrator I spoke with pays editors about $35 PFH. It takes her five-six hours to create one finished hour of audiobook. Included in that time estimate is taking notes, talking with the rights holder, getting advice from other narrators and editors, learning accents and foreign words, doing research, narrating the manuscript, editing, mastering, and loading files. Taking the net of $165 PFH from a $200 PFH job and dividing that by six hours of work gives you an hourly rate of roughly $28.

Can I be an author and a narrator?

Yes, but I think you need separate Amazon logins for ACX.

Some advice for narrators:
I have spent most of my time speaking to authors' needs and concerns, but there's always another side.

How do you handle a demanding author?
If possible, try to avoid entanglements with demanding authors. You may be able to avoid stepping into such a situation if you're communicating well with the author. Most likely, your correspondences will be via email. The author may start out all sugar and sweetness then morph into the customer straight out of the hot place later.

Tips for dealing with demanding rights holders:
- **Set clear expectations ahead of time** – Clear communication can avoid trouble later. Even if problems arise later, you can politely refer the author to earlier correspondences.
  Side note: If an author is making weird demands right away, like the book must be at least a certain of number of hours long, run away from them as fast as you can. You do not want to be boxed in by odd demands.
- **Communicate** – This point kind of touches each of the others. I'm not saying that a demanding rights holder is your fault, but if it's a complete shock to you, there's been a breakdown in communication to date. I don't like phone conversations, so I try to handle everything via email. If you happen to like phone conversations and the author is willing to take a call from you, clear the air that way. It's much quicker than back and forth emails.
- **Educate the author on the behind the scenes portion of your job** – Most people who aren't narrators have zero clue about what goes into a finished hour of audiobook. If the author is being unrealistic, they need to know that.
- **Compromise** – Pick several of the points the author is advocating for and make the adjustments. Leave the rest unchanged but not unaddressed. You need to justify your

nonaction to the rights holder, or they'll nag you about it, thinking you simply forgot.

- **Evaluate the situation** – Breaking the contract should never be your first-tier option, but if the rights holder is desperately clinging to their irrational demands, you may have to for your health and happiness. You do not want to build a reputation as somebody who doesn't finish projects, but you also don't want one project consuming you day and night for an indeterminate amount of time.

Is it better to offer (or work for) a flat fee/per-project stipend/lump sum?

Depends on your point of view. Usually, no. The logic is sound from an outsider-looking-in point of view, but there are very good reasons the industry rarely works this way. It's natural to want to know what your overall costs will be. However, unless the flat fee is extremely high, there's an excellent chance of the narrator becoming frustrated with the project. The narrator would have to be very good at estimating the time and effort required to make the book. The most likely scenario would have them feeling overworked and underpaid.

If you accurately estimate how long the audiobook will be PFH should work fine. You should know how much a project should cost before going in so you can budget properly and offer a fair rate. The narrator will be doing similar reverse calculations to figure out what the PFH or flat fee will work out to in amount per hour of work. Regardless of the fee structure, the project can always run longer than expected. You could still end up frustrated.

Non-exhaustive list of hot-button topics:
Having a final, polished manuscript:

Ideally, the manuscript should be complete and polished. Everybody connected to the indie world understands that sometimes, mistakes slip through because the quality control is only as good as the author is willing to pay for. Authors are by nature tinkerers, so most could be altering things left and right endlessly. Once you make the move to audiobook though, keep changes to a bare minimum.

Nobody has complained to my face about making changes to the audiobook because I made a mistake in the manuscript. But I can certainly see where narrators feel put-upon if they have to edit the grammar as they go to figure out how to read the manuscript properly. Most can avoid the issue by checking the manuscript ahead of agreeing to the project.

I understand that authors are excited to finish their projects. Reading something aloud is one of the best ways to catch mistakes. I think both sides can agree that the story should be the best it can be. The author responsibility then turns to taking the time to do one more sweep before seeking a narrator.

Audiobook cover issues:

- **Audiobook cover size and appearance** – You may have noticed that audiobook covers are squares. ACX has some specific requirements for audiobook covers in terms of look and size. Because ACX covers need to be square shaped, they will naturally be different than the ebook or paperback covers. If you have the skill to make the changes yourself, awesome. If you don't, hiring somebody to make the changes is pretty cheap because the switches are easy if you have the right editing tools.
- **Including the narrator's name** – I've always had my narrator's name included on the covers, but from what I hear, that's not something all rights holders do. I see no reason not to include their name. You hired them for a reason. If the person has their own following, it may even help you capitalize on sales. The easiest way to accomplish this while avoiding the issue of commissioning a whole new cover is to add a sidebar that includes the narrator's name. I heard a rumor that ACX doesn't like those covers, but I've always done it.

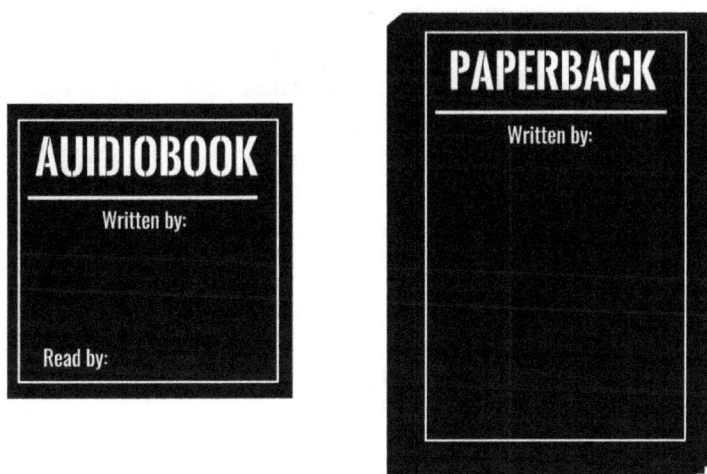

Amazon-specific programs:

- **Whispersync** – This program has been around for a while. Your ebook and audiobook should be very similar. If there's enough match, Amazon will automatically include it in Whispersync. As a reader, it's convenient because you can grab the ebook and the audiobook and have them always automatically sync across multiple devices. Owning the ebook—even a free one—will also give you a steep discount on the audiobook version. As an author, that's great because it encourages people to buy both versions. In a RS deal, it's not so great for the narrator because the royalties still get split as a percentage of the final sale. So, if the audiobook is selling for dirt cheap, you get a fraction of that as your cut. To my knowledge, there's no option for opting out of Whispersync. You could always ask Amazon's customer service.
- **Audible Escape** – From time to time, Amazon will rename this program. It's essentially a subscription program where the reader can listen to unlimited audiobooks of a certain genre, usually romance. I believe authors opt into the program. I've always been leery of it, but since I don't

write in that genre, it's more of an academic concern. From what I'm hearing from authors and narrators who opted in, they regret it ultimately because the sales would have generated more income than the share of the fund Amazon allots to the program. Authors and narrators in RS would get a small amount of money for each minute of their title listened to by the customer.

Key point: I'm hearing almost unanimously from narrators that this program is financial death to RS projects.

Responsibility for audiobook marketing efforts:

The responsibility falls to the author or rights holder. In PFH deals, the narrator ceases to get paid. If the narrator is experienced, he or she may have dozens or hundreds of titles. It's not realistic to believe they're going to want to promote your shiny new audiobook as enthusiastically as you want them to. That said, I've never had a narrator balk at doing interviews or going on blog tours. It's bad form to ask a narrator to pay for any promotional opportunities. In RS and RS$^+$ deals, the narrator has a vested interest in obtaining more sales, but they need to balance that with time spent recording new books.

Conclusion:

Although the financial concerns may differ, I think authors and narrators have the same goal: create an awesome audiobook. When in doubt, ask questions. There is no shame in not knowing something, but keep an open mind and try to see things from the other perspective as you consider audiobook matters. Good luck. I hope you enjoy every step of the audiobook creation experience.

Appendix I:
Sample Invitations

One of the personalized invitations sent for Money Makes it Deadlier:

Hi,

I heard your audition for Fatal Interest, and even though you weren't quite right for that, I would like to personally invite you to audition for Money Makes it Deadlier. This is a separate series about a young, female FBI agent who gets into all sorts of trouble.

Project can be found here:

The unfortunate nature of this business means that I audition/interview dozens of highly talented, wonderful people and get to hire only one at a time.

Auditions should stay open about a week, but if it's anything like Fatal Interest and generates auditions crazy fast, it might be a struggle to keep it open that long. To that end, if it gets near the deadline and you think I'll close the auditions before you're ready, please shoot me a message so I can wait for you.

Thanks for your time.

Sincerely,

Julie C. Gilbert

General invitation left in the additional comments section of ACX:

Hello,

Thank you for the interest in this project. All ladies are welcomed to audition, but please keep in mind that I have already invited about 15 hot contenders for the title. This book has series potential, so I'm looking for a long-term yet flexible partnership here.

I offer hybrid projects with $100 PFH base plus bonuses. We can discuss more details if you win. I hope to keep the auditions open about a week from the start but given that I got 30 auditions for the last project, it may close earlier than anticipated.

Good luck.

Sincerely,

Julie C. Gilbert

Appendix II:
Sample of Audiobook Notes

Money Makes it Deadlier Audiobook Notes

Color Key: (It's so much prettier with the actual colors.)
Purple text: I loved it.
Dark green text: General comment
Light blue text: Explanatory comment
Orange text: Possible mistake – please check
Red text: Definitely hearing something amiss – please change

Notes:

Chapter 8: It's Only a Few Hours
Orange text: 1:02 "Now, Katelyn. (*light blue text*: More emphasis on now…it's a demand. Sorry. Hard to convey that in the dialogue) (picture it like Now. Full stop, Katelyn…sort of let some of the exasperation show through)
Purple text: Rest sounds fine on first listen.

Chapter 9: Much More Exciting
Orange text: 1:34 Noticing the Financial Adviser was (*light blue text*: word change noticing to noting; If you stick with noting, add the word that…or switch back to noticing)
Red text 4:58 settled in Mr. Sims's office, (*light blue text*: it sounds like it's missing the 's here. What do you think? It's a slight technical difference. Grammatically, it changed so that the 's is needed…. but people should still get the point, right? I guess, change it…otherwise they'll think his normal name is Sim; sorry, processing through writing)
Red text: Mr. Sims's office ~6:00; Mr. Sims's ~8:40; 12:10 Mr. Sims's disgruntled
Purple text: Stupid question! Stupid question! (Great inflection) I really like the inflection choices on the normal narration sections.

Resources Page:

Resources Referenced:

ACX's official pitch for Royalty Share Plus:
https://blog.acx.com/2019/06/11/negotiate-your-perfect-deal-with-royalty-share-plus/

Jeffrey Kaffer's blog post about things that annoy narrators:
https://myvoicetalent.wordpress.com/2014/08/10/how-to-make-sure-you-never-find-a-narrator-for-your-audiobook/

Aven Shore's blog post on what makes a narrator happy:
https://www.avenshore.com/blog/2017/6/3/how-to-be-a-star-rights-holder

My blog post on ACX vs. Findaway Voices:
Be aware that some of the information here is outdated.
https://wp.me/p8vm4j-gQ

Other Recommended Resources:

http://www.karencommins.com/narrator-blog

Thank You for Reading:

Creating audiobooks can be a very rewarding experience. I hope you found something useful in this book. If you've enjoyed this book, please consider leaving a review as that will help others find it.

Check out some of my other works. Much of it is clean fiction, though there's also a book about improving your book descriptions. That's called *5 Steps to Better Blurbs*. As you might guess, it's available as an ebook, paperback, or audiobook.

Visit my website (www.juliecgilbert.com) for audiobook samples, book descriptions, playlist links, and a peek at the pretty covers. I still have a lot of audiobook free codes for nearly every title, so please feel free to inquire if that interests you.

If you have questions or randomly need a sympathetic stranger to talk to, feel free to reach out via email.

juliecgilbert5steps@gmail.com or devyaschildren@gmail.com

Sincerely,

Julie C. Gilbert

www.ingramcontent.com/pod-product-compliance
Lightning Source LLC
Chambersburg PA
CBHW061746020426

42331CB00006B/1371